Mag. Claudia Lichtenwagner

AF144015

SMILE 3

Listening Comprehensions

Hörverständnis-Übungen für die

3. Klasse Mittelschule / AHS

G&G

Von Claudia Lichtenwagner bisher im G&G Verlag erschienen:

Smile Listening Comprehensions 1 (978-3-7074-1978-8)
Smile Listening Comprehensions 2 (978-3-7074-2061-6)
Smile Listening Comprehensions 3 (978-3-7074-2184-2)
Smile Listening Comprehensions 4 (978-3-7074-2187-3)

Smile 1 Grammar (978-3-7074-1306-9)
Smile 2 Grammar (978-3-7074-1307-6)
Smile 3 Grammar (978-3-7074-1308-3)
Smile 4 Grammar (978-3-7074-1309-0)

Smile Reading Comprehensions 1 (978-3-7074-1354-0)
Smile Reading Comprehensions 2 (978-3-7074-1508-7)
Smile Reading Comprehensions 3 (978-3-7074-1624-4)
Smile Reading Comprehensions 4 (978-3-7074-1846-0)

Smile Matura-Trainer Speaking Competences (978-3-7074-2080-7)

Sourire 1 (978-3-7074-1310-6)
Sourire 2 (978-3-7074-1311-3)
Sourire 3 (978-3-7074-1312-0)
Sourire 4 (978-3-7074-1313-7)
Sourire 5 (978-3-7074-1314-4)

www.ggverlag.at

ISBN 978-3-7074-2184-2

In der aktuell gültigen Rechtschreibung

4. Auflage 2024

CD aufgenommen im Tonstudio: Walter Till, www.euroacoustics.at
SprecherInnen: Mia Heck, Eddie McLachlan, Bryan Benner, Kathy Nicholson
Aufnahmeleitung und Mischung: Walter Till

Druck und Bindung: Imprint, Ljubljana

VORWORT

Liebe Schülerin, lieber Schüler!

Durch das oftmalige Anhören der Texte, die von Sprecherinnen und Sprechern mit englischer Muttersprache vorgetragen werden, wirst du deine Sprachkenntnisse ständig erweitern. Dein Wortschatz wird anwachsen und es wird dir immer weniger Probleme bereiten, Gehörtes zu verstehen.

Die Hörtexte sind anspruchsvoller und erfordern längere Konzentrationsfähigkeit, die Aufgabenstellungen sind etwas schwieriger als in den ersten beiden Werken.

In diesem Band begegnest du Beiträgen zu folgenden Themen:
Musik, Filme und Regisseure, seltsame Begebenheiten, Ferien, Sehenswürdigkeiten, andere Kulturen, Probleme, Naturkatastrophen, Freundschaft, sich für etwas engagieren, Vorbilder und vieles mehr.

Verschiedene Aufgabenstellungen wie True / False-Entscheidungen, Sätze verbinden, Einfüllübungen, aus verschiedenen Vorschlägen die richtige Lösung auswählen, Fragen beantworten etc. werden dir helfen, neue Vokabel und Satzstrukturen zu erlernen.

Ab Seite 35 befinden sich die Abschriften der gesprochenen Texte, die Vokabeltabellen und die Lösungen aller Aufgabenstellungen.

Weiterhin viel Freude und Erfolg beim Üben!
Prof. Mag. Claudia Lichtenwagner

SMILE – die erfolgreichste Englisch-Lernhilfenreihe
jetzt auch online auf ✅ **edu**active

➤ Über 6.500 interaktive Übungen zu allen Grammatik-Themen
➤ Wiederholung, Testvorbereitung und Hausaufgaben mit automatisierten Auswertungen zur Selbstüberprüfung
➤ https://eduactive.at/reihen/smile-englisch-grammatik

Contents

1 Listen to Oliver talking about his favourite singer and **circle** (kreise ein) **T** (True) or **F** (False):

Track 1

1. Roberta Morris is Oliver's favourite pop singer.	T / F
2. She is twice the age of Oliver.	T / F
3. She is 28 and was born in Miami.	T / F
4. Roberta is married to the soul singer Adam Jones.	T / F
5. Her voice is loud and clear.	T / F
6. She sings about all kinds of problems.	T / F
7. Her songs have got excellent lyrics and a good beat.	T / F
8. Oliver and his brother want to buy all her CDs one day.	T / F
9. Oliver's brother has the same taste in music as Oliver.	T / F
10. The boys always listen to their CDs before doing their homework.	T / F

2 Listen to the interview with Lionel talking about his favourite song and **tick** (kreuze an) **the correct answers**:

Track 2

1. Lionel's favourite song is
   a. ☐ *Never Ever Give Up.*
   b. ☐ *Never Give Up.*
   c. ☐ *Give Up.*

2. The music style he likes best is
   a. ☐ free jazz.
   b. ☐ soul.
   c. ☐ techno.

3. He thinks the melody is
   a. ☐ awful.
   b. ☐ awesome.
   c. ☐ terrible.

4. The song is about
   a. ☐ a boy who is liked by everyone.
   b. ☐ a really nasty boy.
   c. ☐ an outsider.
   d. ☐ a married woman.

5. The girl
   a. ☐ also bullied him.
   b. ☐ was nasty to him.
   c. ☐ married the boy later.

6. At the class reunion he sees that
   a. ☐ he is the only winner.
   b. ☐ he is still bullied.
   c. ☐ he is a loser.

7. The lyrics are
   a. ☐ comfortable.
   b. ☐ comforting.
   c. ☐ meaningless.

8. Ken Mars has got a
   a. ☐ clear voice.
   b. ☐ unique voice.
   c. ☐ rough voice.
   d. ☐ soft voice.

3 Listen to Elisa talking about her taste in music and **match** (füge zusammen) **the sentence halves** (die Satzhälften):

Track 3

1. Elisa is into dancing and is highly interested
2. She thinks the beat in a song must be
3. She likes a strong rhythm with
4. Elisa says that Phil Collins does some
5. The drummer of Santana is
6. Deep Purple and Chicago are world-famous
7. They are old bands but they
8. For every song Elisa has got
9. Her friends say that she is an
10. Elisa wants to be a professional

a. fantastic too.
b. for their drum solos.
c. in a good melody.
d. extremely good dancer.
e. long drum solos.
f. really great drum solos.
g. different moves.
h. dancer one day.
i. are great and skilled.
j. electrifying.

4 Listen to Joe talking about music and **circle T** or **F**:

Track 4

1. Joe hasn't got a favourite band but he has got a song he likes best. T / F
2. He likes music videos and he wants to know what the stars look like. T / F
3. Joe listens to songs because of their message. T / F
4. What he really likes in a song is the rhythm and a strong beat. T / F
5. He adores guitar solos because he is a guitarist himself. T / F
6. He thinks Knopfler is one of the best guitar players in the world. T / F
7. With his guitar he can create strong emotions in his listeners. T / F
8. He likes to forget everything around him when listening to music. T / F

5 Listen to the two judges on the TV show *The Next Top Pop Band* and **circle T** or **F**:

Track 5

1. One girl forgot the lyrics and sang "lalala". T / F
2. Then the band stopped singing. T / F
3. Their moves were clumsy and wooden. T / F
4. One guy stepped on the girl's toes. T / F
5. One girl bumped into the boy dancing in the middle. T / F
6. Some members of the band can't sing well. T / F
7. There were too many high and deep notes in their song. T / F
8. One judge thinks they can win the competition. T / F
9. The band was dressed in green leather jackets. T / F
10. One judge thinks that the audience will like the band's performance. T / F

6 Listen to the two critics on the TV show. **Fill in the words** you hear:

Track 6

1. That was ....!
2. It was a b............................. p............................. .
3. You have got ....
4. You are an .... singer.
5. You've got a ...., strong .... and you weren't .... even in the most d............................. s............................. .
6. You chose an .... song.
7. You are going to .... it, that's for ....

7 Listen to the latest interview with Cathy Clarkson, a pop singer, and **tick** (kreuze an) **the answers that are NOT correct**:

Track 7

1. How has Cathy's life changed?
   a. ☐ She is famous now.
   b. ☐ She goes on tours.
   c. ☐ She has good grades.
   d. ☐ Fans follow her.

2. The price of fame is that she
   a. ☐ has no friends.
   b   ☐ is surrounded by fans.
   c. ☐ needs bodyguards.
   d. ☐ has to work hard.

3. For her success she has to
   a. ☐ rehearse a lot.
   b. ☐ study a lot.
   c. ☐ write songs.
   d. ☐ produce a new album.

4. How did her classmates react?
   a. ☐ Some helped her.
   b. ☐ Some were envious.
   c. ☐ Some sent her schoolwork.
   d. ☐ They didn't like her.

5. Other classmates
   a. ☐ lied to her.
   b. ☐ were jealous.
   c. ☐ spread rumours.
   d. ☐ were nasty to her.

6. Cathy wanted to finish school
   a. ☐ with good marks.
   b. ☐ with As.
   c. ☐ without cheating.
   d   ☐ as soon as possible.

7. Her plans for the future are to
   a. ☐ finish her studies.
   b. ☐ get married.
   c. ☐ have two children.
   d. ☐ buy a house in Paris.

8. Her advice for others:
   a. ☐ Follow your hearts.
   b. ☐ You must love fame.
   c. ☐ Be ambitious.
   d. ☐ Be hard-working.

8   Listen to Raymond's story and **circle T** or **F**:

Track 8

1.	Raymond was rather superstitious and was afraid of Friday 13th.	T / F
2.	Last year there was a Friday 13th where lots of things went wrong.	T / F
3.	In the morning he jumped out of bed and fell over his dog.	T / F
4.	He twisted his ankle and ran into the bathroom.	T / F
5.	He dropped his cup of coffee because it was so hot.	T / F
6.	His trousers and his sweater were covered in coffee then.	T / F
7.	He had to change his clothes.	T / F
8.	He missed his bus for school and his mum took him to school by car.	T / F
9.	On their way to school they had an accident because of a black cat.	T / F
10.	Raymond fell asleep during a lesson.	T / F
11.	In the break he bit his lip while he was eating his sandwich.	T / F
12.	On his way home from school there was a thunderstorm.	T / F
13.	He deleted an important file from his computer.	T / F
14.	Raymond fancied Linda very much.	T / F
15.	He sometimes asked Linda for a date.	T / F
16.	When she came to borrow his Math books he hugged her.	T / F

9   Listen to Mr Hall talking about a very strange thing that happened to him and **circle T** or **F**:

Track 9

1.	Mr Hall sold his house in Fairwater Street.	T / F
2.	He wanted to have a farm with cows, chickens, corn and vegetables.	T / F
3.	His family didn't like his plan at all.	T / F
4.	One day, on his way home he saw a bar he had never seen before.	T / F
5.	He decided to have a beer and stay at the bar until the rain was over.	T / F
6.	He knew a lot of the guests there.	T / F
7.	Back home he couldn't put his key into the lock.	T / F
8.	A different family, named Cunnington, lived in his house.	T / F
9.	An old lady invited him into the house and told him a funny story.	T / F
10.	Mr Hall thought that he was caught in the wrong time.	T / F
11.	The old woman sent Mr Hall to the baker's.	T / F
12.	She told him why she knew about his visit to the bar.	T / F
13.	Mr Hall couldn't find the bar any more.	T / F
14.	His neighbour Bill took Mr Hall home in his car.	T / F
15.	When Mr Hall came home he said that they were not going to move.	T / F
16.	Mr Hall told his family about the strange incident at once.	T / F

10 Listen to Liam talking about how he got to know his girlfriend and **tick the correct options** (Möglichkeiten):

Track 10

1. Liam was on a holiday in Italy with
   a. ☐ his best friend.
   b. ☐ his parents.
   c. ☐ some friends.

2. They enjoyed
   a. ☐ sleeping at the beach.
   b. ☐ swimming in the pool.
   c. ☐ playing volleyball.

3. One day Liam stepped on a
   a. ☐ golden earring.
   b. ☐ shell.
   c. ☐ sharp stone.

4. He hurt
   a. ☐ his ankle.
   b. ☐ the sole of his foot.
   c. ☐ his toe.

5. He went to
   a. ☐ the manager of the hotel.
   b. ☐ the receptionist.
   c. ☐ his best friend.

6. The earrings were a present from
   a. ☐ the girl's parents.
   b. ☐ the girl's mother.
   c. ☐ the girl's grandmother.

7. The earrings were golden
   a. ☐ with a blue stone.
   b. ☐ with a green stone.
   c. ☐ with a red stone.

8. She invited Liam
   a. ☐ to dinner.
   b. ☐ for an ice cream.
   c. ☐ to lunch.

11 Listen to Rose talking about how she found the man of her dreams and **fill in the missing words**:

1. Rose normally doesn't .... in horoscopes.
2. She went to see a friend in .... to .... for an exam.
3. She wanted to .... a street and stepped onto the pedestrian ....
4. A car .... the red light and .... her over.
5. She had a horrible .... in her .... foot and arm.
6. There was .... on her new ....
7. She passed .... and when she came .... again, her arm and her leg were in .... and there was a .... around her head.
8. Just before .... , a .... doctor came into her room.
9. He was the doctor in .... for that night.
10. She got to know the man of her .... So the horoscope didn't lie.

5

12 Listen to Jonathan talking about the nice coincidence that changed his life and **match the sentence halves:**

Track 12

1. It sometimes happens that	a. excellent wines.
2. This was the case on Jonathan's	b. enjoyed dinner together.
3. The airline needed two volunteers who	c. sightseeing together.
4. The airline offered a great hotel and a	d. had a lot in common.
5. Jonathan and a young lady agreed to	e. flight to New York.
6. They were taken to their hotel by taxi and	f. next to each other.
7. They had a delicious dinner with	g. would take a later flight.
8. They talked a lot and noticed that they	h. take a later flight.
9. The following day they sat on the plane	i. lovely candlelight dinner.
10. In New York they did a lot of	j. a plane is overbooked.

13 Listen to Jill talking about how she found the boy of her dreams and **tick the correct answers:**

Track 13

1. Jill spent her holidays with her cousin Norah
   a. ☐ at the sea.
   b. ☐ in the mountains.
   c. ☐ at a lake.

2. They spent their afternoons
   a. ☐ sleeping in the sun.
   b. ☐ reading in the sun.
   c. ☐ talking about their problems.
   d. ☐ sleeping in the sand.

3. During the rowing boat trip Jill found a
   a. ☐ bottle.
   b. ☐ piece of wood.
   c. ☐ dead fish.

4. In the bottle there was
   a. ☐ some sand.
   b. ☐ a sheet of paper.
   c. ☐ some water.
   d. ☐ some wine.

5. The letter was an invitation for a
   a. ☐ candlelight dinner.
   b. ☐ lunch at a bar.
   c. ☐ drink at a bar.

6

14 Listen to the phone-in show and **circle T** or **F**:

Track 14

1.	Something strange happened to her which made her believe in angels.	T / F
2.	She was on her way home from a pop concert.	T / F
3.	She saw an old woman carrying two heavy bags.	T / F
4.	The old lady lived in flat number 13 on the second floor.	T / F
5.	The lady invited Mary-Ann for a cup of coffee and some biscuits.	T / F
6.	The biscuits were old and hard.	T / F
7.	The lady talked a lot about her life which was very interesting.	T / F
8.	Mary-Ann forgot about the time and had to hurry to the entrance.	T / F
9.	When she arrived, the entrance was closed and she couldn't get in.	T / F
10.	She was very angry and took the bus to visit her friend Lucy.	T / F
11.	Lucy told her about the explosion near the entrance of the stadium.	T / F
12.	Mary-Ann quickly called her parents to tell them that she was safe.	T / F
13.	The next day she wanted to visit the old lady again to thank her.	T / F
14.	Mary-Ann couldn't find flat number 13 again.	T / F
15.	Somebody told her that the old lady died in a fire many years ago.	T / F
16.	Mary-Ann put the flowers on the old lady's grave.	T / F

15 Listen to Jeremy talking about his favourite holidays and **circle T** or **F**:

Track 15

1.	His favourite holiday was at a mountain hut with his family.	T / F
2.	They had to leave the car one hundred meters below the hut.	T / F
3.	Their dad said they should not take too many things with them.	T / F
4.	Jeremy and his brother shared a big room with a bunk-bed in it.	T / F
5.	In the bathroom there were two basins and a tub.	T / F
6.	There was no running water so they got water from a well.	T / F
7.	They had candles for the evening since there was no electricity.	T / F
8.	Their neighbours were chickens, sheep and cows.	T / F
9.	It was a bit boring for them because their mobile phones didn't work.	T / F
10.	They had to cut wood for the stove.	T / F
11.	They went to the nearest supermarket to buy the food they needed.	T / F
12.	The boys didn't want to play with the cat because it scratched them.	T / F
13.	The cat played with small plastic balls, which the boys threw away.	T / F
14.	Jeremy and his brother played a lot of games together.	T / F
15.	In the evenings they sang songs in front of an open fire.	T / F
16.	His dad promised them to go there again next year.	T / F

16   Listen to the children talking about their holidays and **circle T** or **F**:

Track 16

1. Emily is into mountain climbing and she's really good at it.   T / F
2. The equipment for her hobby is not cheap.   T / F
3. She did a course two years ago and now she climbs every free minute.   T / F
4. Samuel likes visiting towns because he loves sightseeing.   T / F
5. He collects recipes in every country and has got a large collection.   T / F
6. He wants to write a book on cooking one day.   T / F
7. Laura and her parents are skiers.   T / F
8. Her brother is into snowboarding.   T / F
9. In the summertime they like going camping at the sea.   T / F
10. They love hiking in the mountains and having a meal at an alpine hut.   T / F

17   Listen to the interview with Ken about his year in India and **tick** the sentences that do **NOT belong in** (dazugehören) the interview:

Track 17

1. Ken has always been interested in that country.   ☐
2. He wanted to get in touch with Indian customs.   ☐
3. Ken wanted to spend some time at the beach of Goa.   ☐
4. He visited about a hundred temples all over the country.   ☐
5. He collected many recipes because he wanted to be a cook.   ☐
6. One day somebody stole all his bags.   ☐
7. He worked as a shop assistant and as a guide.   ☐
8. In the south it was hot; in the north it was cold.   ☐
9. In the north he worked as a tea leaves picker.   ☐
10. He worked as a cook in an Indian restaurant in Delhi.   ☐
11. When the monsoon flooded a town, he had to take a boat.   ☐
12. Rain like that flooded a town in less than half an hour.   ☐
13. After a monsoon shower his flight was delayed by four hours.   ☐
14. He travelled around by train, plane, bus and on lorries.   ☐
15. Once he had to sit on the load area of a lorry.   ☐
16. There weren't many people on the lorry.   ☐
17. There was a cow on the lorry, too.   ☐
18. He was sitting among cages with chickens, rabbits and ducks.   ☐
19. One man had brought half a pig with him.   ☐
20. He was so tired during the trip on the lorry that he fell asleep.   ☐
21. On the lorry it was stinking horribly from sweat and blood.   ☐
22. After the trip he suffered from a terrible back pain.   ☐

18 Listen to Mrs Robinson talking about the worst holiday in her life and **circle T** or **F**:

Track 18

1.	They booked a hotel at the sea and rented a car for two weeks.	T / F
2.	During the flight she suffered from altitude sickness.	T / F
3.	The catalogue promised that the hotel was nice.	T / F
4.	They arrived and moved into their hotel room at once.	T / F
5.	While they were waiting for the room they went swimming.	T / F
6.	The room was awfully dirty with cockroaches, hairs and dust.	T / F
7.	Then they complained about the dirt to the headmaster.	T / F
8.	The manager cleaned the floor and changed the bed linen.	T / F
9.	Breakfast was good with bacon and eggs, fruits and sparkling wine.	T / F
10.	They spent nice hours at the sea reading and swimming.	T / F
11.	They also did some sightseeing in the neighbouring town.	T / F
12.	On the last day of their holiday their neighbour had an accident.	T / F
13.	They had an accident and crashed into the back of a bus.	T / F
14.	Mr Robinson was severely injured and had to stay in hospital.	T / F
15.	Mr Robinson had a broken shoulder and a broken thighbone.	T / F
16.	Mrs Robinson only had some bruises.	T / F
17.	After five weeks the Robinsons flew home together.	T / F

19 Listen to the children talking about a film on dangerous animals and **tick the correct answers**:

Track 19

1. At the cinema the children saw
   a. ☐ an awful film.
   b. ☐ an awesome film.
   c. ☐ a boring film.

2. The scenes in the film were of
   a. ☐ biting.
   b. ☐ climbing.
   c. ☐ hunting and eating.

3. A bear climbs …….. a monkey.
   a. ☐ faster than
   b. ☐ as fast as
   c. ☐ not as fast as

4. The snake tried to swallow a
   a. ☐ crocodile.
   b. ☐ pig.
   c. ☐ monkey.

5. Cindy …….. the film.
   a. ☐ liked
   b. ☐ recommended
   c. ☐ couldn't recommend

6. *Tiny Grey* is a film for
   a. ☐ the whole family.
   b. ☐ parents only.
   c. ☐ children only.

9

20 Listen to Helen talking about a film and **match the sentence halves:**

Track 20

1. *Happy Feet* is an animated film
2. She went to the cinema with
3. The film is funny and sad at
4. Every penguin has to sing his
5. Little Mumble can't sing but he is able
6. Of course there is a
7. The film is gorgeous and Helen can
8. There are sequels but the first *Happy Feet*

a. heartsong to find a mate.
b. to tap-dance perfectly.
c. warmly recommend it.
d. the same time.
e. is definitely the best.
f. for children and adults.
g. happy ending.
h. her whole family.

21 Listen to the children talking about dangerous animals in the world and **answer the questions:**

Track 21

1. Why are African killer bees so dangerous?

....

....

2. Why are Tse Tse flies and mosquitos so dangerous?

....

3. Why would Brenda not like to meet a hippo or a rhino?

....

4. What else does Brenda tell Mark about rhinos?

....

5. What is a deadly roll?

....

6. What happens if you are bitten by a Black Mamba?

....

7. What happens to the victims of the Carpet Viper?

....

22 Listen to Grace giving a presentation on the Poison Dart frog and **circle the correct options** (Möglichkeiten):

Track 22

1. The Poison Dart frogs count among the *more / most* dangerous animals.
2. The frogs have enough poison to kill *20,000 / 2000* mice.
3. They are *brightly / bright* coloured with beautiful patterns.
4. You can find them in *orange, blue, black, green and red / orange, pink, blue, green and red*.
5. *Scientists / People* think that they become so toxic because of their poisonous *food / foot*.
6. The frogs feed on *poisonous / poison* insects, beetles and ants.
7. They capture their prey with their long and *stinking / sticky* tongues.
8. Frogs in tanks get insects that are not *toxic / toxin*.
9. You can find them *in / on* trees or under stones and leaves.
10. They are only 20 to 40 *millimetres / centimetres* long.
11. Animals *do not eat / eat* them because of their bright colours.
12. The frogs may get very *cold / old* and live from *20 to 120 / 12 to 20* years.
13. Hunters need their *poison / poisonous* for their *arrows / aeroplanes*.
14. They rub the arrow tips on the frogs' *backs / legs*.
15. Their *toxic / toxin* is also used for medicine.
16. Their poison is also used *with / for* medicine.

23 Listen to Lenny talking about Madame Tussauds in London and **circle T or F**:

Track 23

1. Madame Tussauds is one of the most popular tourist attractions.   T / F
2. Madame Tussauds shows wax figures of famous people.   T / F
3. The museum houses the wax figures of politicians and actors.   T / F
4. There is also a collection of superheroes made of wax.   T / F
5. Even the main character of the film *The Hunger Games* is there.   T / F
6. You can also see wax figures of kings and queens in the museum.   T / F
7. The wax figures look very real.   T / F
8. You mustn't take photos of the figures.   T / F
9. If you touch the figures, you must be very careful.   T / F
10. A visit to the Chamber of Horrors is good fun for the whole family.   T / F
11. You can visit wax museums all over the world.   T / F
12. The first waxed figure was created in 1877.   T / F
13. Sometimes the museums are used as settings for films.   T / F

24 Listen to Teresa talking about Lisbon Oceanarium and **circle T** or **F:**

Track 24

1.	Lisbon Oceanarium is the world's largest oceanarium.	T / F
2.	They display fish, birds, seals, penguins and many more species.	T / F
3.	On the right of the oceanarium there is a huge tank.	T / F
4.	The biggest tank is seven meters deep.	T / F
5.	The main attraction is the large sunfish.	T / F
6.	The sunfish has got real lips.	T / F
7.	Around the main tank there are five smaller tanks.	T / F
8.	You get the impression that there are more small tanks.	T / F
9.	The sharks eat smaller fish in the tank.	T / F
10.	Teresa was bored and wanted to leave after two hours.	T / F

25 Listen to Simon's presentation on the Eiffel Tower and **circle T** or **F:**

Track 25

1.	The Eiffel Tower is named after its creator Gustave Eiffel.	T / F
2.	The construction began in 1889.	T / F
3.	Its four levels are accessible for visitors.	T / F
4.	To climb the tower you can use stairs or lifts.	T / F
5.	If you walk, you must climb more than 600 steps to the 2nd platform.	T / F
6.	On the third platform there is a nice restaurant.	T / F
7.	The restaurants are very costly.	T / F
8.	The entire weight of the tower is about 10,000 tons.	T / F
9.	The tower is painted with 60 tons of paint every nine years.	T / F
10.	There is a large TV on top of the tower.	T / F

26 Listen to Sibyl talking about the Globe Theatre and **circle T** or **F:**

Track 26

1.	The Globe Theatre was built by actors in 1599.	T / F
2.	Many of Shakespeare's plays were performed there.	T / F
3.	The theatre was destroyed by a fire when a candle set fire to the roof.	T / F
4.	Many people were killed but the theatre was rebuilt one year later.	T / F
5.	It was very loud during a performance.	T / F
6.	The audience loved battles and fights with sheep's blood.	T / F
7.	At night the stage was lit by candles.	T / F
8.	The new theatre is exactly at the same place where the old one was.	T / F
9.	It was an open-air theatre so the audience got wet in the rain.	T / F
10.	In the more expensive places people had to stand.	T / F

27 Listen to a tour guide giving a presentation on the Statue of Liberty and **tick the correct options** (Möglichkeiten):

Track 27

1. The statue is situated
   a. ☐ on Liberty Island.
   b. ☐ on New York Island.
   c. ☐ on Harbour Island.

2. It is made
   a. ☐ from iron.
   b. ☐ of wood.
   c. ☐ from copper.

3. It was a gift from
   a. ☐ Italy.
   b. ☐ Germany.
   c. ☐ France.

4. It is holding up a
   a. ☐ flower.
   b. ☐ torch.
   c. ☐ stick.

5. At its feet there is a
   a. ☐ broken glass.
   b. ☐ broken vase.
   c. ☐ broken chain.

6. The statue and the pedestal
   a. ☐ are 93 m high.
   b. ☐ are 46 m high.
   c. ☐ are 204 m high.

7. Its total weight is
   a. ☐ 240 tons.
   b. ☐ 204 tons.
   c. ☐ 244 tons.

8. Only .... visitors are allowed to visit the statue a day.
   a. ☐ 240
   b. ☐ 204
   c. ☐ 244

9. You can take .... with you onto the statue.
   a. ☐ an umbrella
   b. ☐ a camera and pills.
   c. ☐ a bag.

28   Listen to Carla talking about superstition and circle T or F:

Track 28

1.	Carla is superstitious because she believes in curses and spells.	T / F
2.	She did well in her job interview and got the job she applied for.	T / F
3.	Two brothers who worked in the office helped her a lot.	T / F
4.	They spread rumours about Carla that were completely untrue.	T / F
5.	The brothers didn't want anybody to talk to Carla.	T / F
6.	Carla enjoyed her further training.	T / F
7.	The brothers tried to disturb Carla's presentation.	T / F
8.	She took revenge and put a spell on them.	T / F
9.	She imagined them sitting in a wheelchair.	T / F
10.	Her curse didn't come true.	T / F
11.	The younger brother suffered a heart attack.	T / F
12.	The older brother fell down a mountain.	T / F

29   Listen to the interview with Tran Duc Thien about superstition in Vietnam and **circle T** or **F**:

Track 29

1.	Vietnamese people express high admiration for a new-born child.	T / F
2.	Devils take handsome boys away.	T / F
3.	A mother says to her son, "My dear ugly baby."	T / F
4.	Every child gets two names: a bad one and a good one.	T / F
5.	Evil spirits are more interested in girls.	T / F
6.	There are often mirrors in the hall of a Vietnamese home.	T / F
7.	They always put at least two bowls of rice on a table.	T / F
8.	One portion of rice is for the neighbours.	T / F
9.	They burn their bikes as presents for the dead relatives.	T / F
10.	The dead people need the same things as we have on earth.	T / F
11.	The New Year festival lasts for three weeks.	T / F
12.	All houses are decorated with flowers and paper lanterns.	T / F
13.	Children get lucky money wrapped in red paper.	T / F
14.	They clap pots and pans together to scare the evil ghosts away.	T / F
15.	They eat sticky rice cake filled with peas and carrots.	T / F
16.	They buy a bag of salt for good luck.	T / F
17.	They must say words like "sad, unhappy, die or evil".	T / F
18.	Housewives clean the floor very carefully during the festival.	T / F
19.	They ask fortune tellers about their future.	T / F
20.	On the first day of the New Year they invite a lucky person over.	T / F

30 Listen to the phone-in show *Ask Everybody* and **fill in the missing words:**

Track 30

1. I have got a real .... with my best friend.
2. Last weekend we .... at a disco.
3. She kissed my .... right in .... of me.
4. I .... with both of them.
5. I don't .... their ....
6. Here is our first ....
7. I would have done the ....
8. They don't deserve your ....
9. Don't be so ....
10. What .... would you like to give to Mandy?
11. There is only one .... to the problem.
12. That's not a good basis for an honest ....

31 Listen to the phone-in radio programme and **circle T** or **F:**

Track 31

1. For Fiona, a good friend is someone she can trust. T / F
2. A good friend stands by her in hard times. T / F
3. A good friend sometimes tells her white lies. T / F
4. Her friend should tell her frankly when she looks awful in a dress. T / F
5. For her, a friend must be reliable and understanding. T / F
6. A good friend doesn't have to listen to you. T / F
7. Simon must have fun with his friend. T / F
8. They must share the same interests. T / F
9. They shouldn't spend too much time together. T / F
10. His friend must keep a secret. T / F
11. He must be discreet and understand Simon's problems. T / F
12. He should be a good skater and be good at riding. T / F
13. He should be keen on playing tennis. T / F
14. He should be able to swim and climb trees. T / F
15. Clarissa needs a helpful friend. T / F
16. Her friend should comfort her when she is down. T / F
17. For Clarissa, a friend must be careful. T / F
18. He or she must stand by her when she needs someone to talk to. T / F
19. A friend mustn't be jealous because that would be a sign of mistrust. T / F
20. Her friend should kiss her. T / F

32 Listen to Adrian and Sally talking about friendship and **tick** the **answers that are NOT correct**:

Track 32

1. Adrian's friend must be
   a. ☐ reasonable.
   b. ☐ reliable.
   c. ☐ a smoker.

2. His friend should
   a. ☐ be fit.
   b. ☐ like sports.
   c. ☐ be fair.
   d. ☐ take drugs.

3. His friend should
   a. ☐ never quarrel.
   b. ☐ be ready to apologize.
   c. ☐ keep their secrets.
   d ☐ not tell their secrets.

4. Sally thinks a best friend must
   a. ☐ give you confidence.
   b. ☐ be on Facebook.
   c. ☐ give you support.

5. She believes best friends
   a. ☐ are not jealous.
   b. ☐ share photos.
   c. ☐ hang out with you.
   d. ☐ share messages.

6. She is of the opinion that friends
   a. ☐ hurt your feelings.
   b. ☐ encourage you.
   c. ☐ congratulate you.
   d. ☐ feel good together.

33 Listen to Lauren giving her opinion on what a best friend means to her and **fill in the missing words**:

Track 33

1. Lauren's best friend should .... for her.
2. She should be .... and supportive.
3. She should be open-minded and take .... of her.
4. A good friend should do .... for her and with her.
5. They should have .... together and she should make her
   ....
6. A real friend always tells the ....
7. She can be herself without having to .... to be somebody
   else.
8. They should like .... things and have the
   .... interests.
9. Her best friend should be .... horses and she should be
   ....
10. That's her .... of a perfect ....

34   Listen to the telephone call between two friends and **circle T** or **F**:

1. Robert is going to have a big, black dragon tattooed on his arm.   T / F
2. April thinks that Robert is crazy.   T / F
3. Robert has asked his parents but they said "no".   T / F
4. April is totally against tattoos.   T / F
5. She says a tattoo destroys the skin and the needle hurts badly.   T / F
6. Robert thinks that a doctor can remove the tattoo.   T / F
7. Robert says that Amanda will like the tattoo.   T / F
8. April is jealous of Amanda.   T / F
9. Robert thanks April for her good advice.   T / F
10. April is a true friend to Robert.   T / F
11. April and Robert have known each other since kindergarten.   T / F
12. She says he should have an earring instead of the tattoo.   T / F
13. Robert and April are still best friends.   T / F

35   Listen to the telephone conversation and **tick the correct answers**:

1. Lara showed Ann
   a. ☐ her school building.
   b. ☐ the ice cream parlour.
   c. ☐ the cinema.
   d. ☐ the park.

2. Ann had a
   a. ☐ birthday party.
   b. ☐ garden party.
   c. ☐ welcoming party.
   d. ☐ dinner party.

3. Ann bought the same
   a. ☐ pink shorts as Lara.
   b. ☐ pink pullover as Lara.
   c. ☐ pink dress as Lara.
   d. ☐ pink jeans as Lara.

4. Lara didn't go to the cinema as
   a. ☐ she was tired.
   b. ☐ she had no time.
   c. ☐ nobody had told her.
   d. ☐ she wasn't interested.

5. The agony aunt tells Lara to
   a. ☐ talk to Ann and her friends together.
   b. ☐ do nothing.
   c. ☐ be mean to Ann.
   d. ☐ sulk.

6. Ann tries
   a. ☐ to be nice to Lara.
   b. ☐ not to be jealous.
   c. ☐ to sort out her problem.
   d. ☐ to buy Lara's friends.

36   Listen to Kim and Carrie who are best friends and **circle T** or **F**:

Track 36

1. Kim and Carrie are sisters and best friends.   T / F
2. They have known each other since kindergarten.   T / F
3. Their mothers found out that they looked a bit similar.   T / F
4. They wear the same tattoos and tongue piercings.   T / F
5. They always spend their holidays together with their families.   T / F
6. They have never had an argument.   T / F
7. Generally, they get on well with each other.   T / F
8. Their boyfriends are twin brothers.   T / F
9. They have got the same taste in boys.   T / F
10. Their mothers also look the same.   T / F

37   Listen to the pupils talking about their favourite film directors and **match the sentence halves**:

Track 37

1. Alfred Hitchcock is called   a. excellent fight scenes.
2. His movies are full of wit and they have   b. of Sci-Fi and war films.
3. Some scenes in his films are so scary that   c. the film-gangsters.
4. His characters have a strange relationship   d. important messages.
5. Hitchcock himself sometimes turns   e. excellent storylines.
6. Ridley Scott is a master of historical drama,   f. money with his films.
7. His films have got great music and   g. the "Master of Suspense".
8. Uprenda's films have got very   h. they make you tremble.
9. He does not want to entertain or make   i. with their mothers.
10. In *Om* real gangsters play the parts of   j. up in a scene.

38   Listen to Max talking about his favourite film and **tick the correct answers**:

Track 38

1. Max's favourite film is about
   a. ☐ a group of girls.
   b. ☐ a group of five boys.
   c. ☐ a group of women.

2. The title of the film is
   a. ☐ well-chosen.
   b. ☐ stupid.
   c. ☐ misleading.

3. The group helps
   a. ☐ the police.
   b. ☐ other children.
   c. ☐ mostly girls.

4. There is a
   a. ☐ witty ending.
   b. ☐ sad ending.
   c. ☐ happy ending.

39 Listen to Katie talking about her favourite film and **circle the correct options** (Möglichkeiten):

Track 39

1. Katie's favourite film is a *horror thriller* / *a detective film*.
2. The *headmaster* / *director* used lots of special effects.
3. He filmed the most horrible scenes in *black and white* / *grey and white*.
4. The *screenplay* / *play* was gripping and *scary* / *scared*.
5. No second of the film was *bored* / *boring*.
6. Sometimes something *quiet* / *quite* unusual happened.
7. Sophia Lansbury has become a very successful *star* / *singer*.
8. She was so good-looking with her *white* / *weird* face.
9. If somebody opens the box, he will find a normal, *woollen* / *wooden* doll.
10. When it is dark the doll comes to *live* / *life*.
11. She takes terrible revenge on *people* / *pupils* who are not nice to children.
12. You follow her thoughts and kind of *enter* / *entertain* her brain.
13. The music is *awful* / *awesome*, too.
14. You are always *surprising* / *surprised* about what comes next.
15. The nursery rhyme ends up in a shrill *sound* / *song*.
16. The viewers must be *over 16* / *under 16*.

40 Listen to Emma talking about her favourite video game and **circle T** or **F**:

Track 40

1. Emma's favourite video game is *Shangri-La* which means "peace". T / F
2. The game has got excellent graphics and the people look so real. T / F
3. In the game you have to defeat enemies. T / F
4. It came out for the first time in January 2018. T / F
5. The sounds of the game are great, no boring "bleep, bleep". T / F
6. Emma thinks the game will be very successful. T / F
7. When playing it you must be fast and have perfect concentration. T / F
8. You have to be good at climbing and mountain biking. T / F
9. You have to shoot very quickly. T / F
10. What she likes best about the game is that there are gushes of blood. T / F
11. You have to buy points and useful keys. T / F
12. The aim of this game is to destroy the kingdom of darkness. T / F
13. You create a new paradise by saving people and animals. T / F
14. There is no time limit in the game so you can play it endlessly. T / F
15. There is no danger of getting hooked on the game. T / F
16. The creator of the game gives one third of his income to help people. T / F

41 Listen to the radio programme *Teens Speak Out* **and answer the questions:**

Track 41

1. What is the best thing for Holly about being 13?

....

2. What does she spend her money on?

....

3. What does she save part of her money for?

....

4. When has she got to be at home in the evening?

....

5. What does Holly do with her Facebook friends?

....

6. Why is she not allowed to meet her contacts without asking her parents?

....

7. Who was "the cool guy", her friend Elisa wanted to meet, in reality?

....

8. What is Holly allowed to buy alone?

....

9. Why is she so happy to buy her own clothes?

....

10. What is Holly not allowed to stuff herself with?

....

11. What is she not allowed to have without asking her parents first?

....

12. What is she allowed to do when her parents or her friends' parents are in?

....

42   Listen to Riley and **tick what he is allowed to do:**

Track 42

1. stay up later   ☐
2. go to the cinema with friends   ☐
3. stay out after nine   ☐
4. watch late-night films   ☐
5. watch a football match with his brother   ☐
6. invite friends to their house   ☐
7. cook with his friends   ☐
8. drink alcohol   ☐
9. use his parents' camera   ☐
10. stuff himself with sweets   ☐
11. eat hamburgers twice a week   ☐
12. play video games up to two hours a day   ☐
13. wear an earring   ☐
14. listen to loud music when his parents are home   ☐
15. hang out with kids his parents do not know   ☐

43   Listen to Ruby talking about her family and **match the sentence halves:**

Track 43

1. Ruby is not allowed to enter the living   a. the kitchen must be clean.
2. The shoes must be left in   b. barbecues in the garden.
3. They are not allowed to make a mess   c. six or seven p.m.
4. When her mum comes home from work,   d. be clean.
5. They mustn't eat in the living room or   e. weed and mow the grass.
6. They only eat in the dining room   f. the hall.
7. In the summertime they often have   g. stains or scribbling.
8. They have to clean out the cage of their   h. room with shoes on.
9. They have to help in   i. where the roses grow.
10. They have to water the flowers,   j. school things.
11. Their parents come home as late as   k. the garden.
12. They are not allowed to play ball games   l. or in the kitchen.
13. Their parents are strict about the girls'   m. up in their rooms.
14. Their books and notebooks must   n. in the kitchen.
15. Their books must not have dog-ears,   o. about their school things.
16. Their dad hates when they are careless   p. budgie regularly.

44 Listen to the radio programme *Meet the World* and **circle T** or **F:**

Track 44

1.	Samuel mostly lives in the same way as his great-grandfather did.	T / F
2.	He has got a TV at home and lots of video games.	T / F
3.	At school there is a computer and the Internet.	T / F
4.	He sometimes thinks his life is a bit boring.	T / F
5.	Samuel has got a lot of work at school and on his farm.	T / F
6.	They have got one tractor, some cars and lots of horses.	T / F
7.	Most important in their group is the family and the community.	T / F
8.	He wants to join the army one day.	T / F
9.	Samuel is interested in the latest fashions.	T / F
10.	The girls never cut or dye their hair.	T / F
11.	The girls wear rings, bracelets and necklaces.	T / F
12.	Most men in his community wear long beards.	T / F
13.	He has got four brothers and one sister.	T / F
14.	His mother tongue is Pennsylvania German.	T / F
15.	When he is older he will spend one year in San Francisco.	T / F
16.	After that year he will stay in the modern world.	T / F
17.	He wants to have a restaurant for the tourists that come to his village.	T / F

45 Listen to the phone-in show *Meet the World* and **circle T** or **F:**

Track 45

1.	Benan is the Australian Aboriginal name for Toby.	T / F
2.	Benan is an Aboriginal boy and lives in Sydney.	T / F
3.	Some of his people live in the Southern Territory.	T / F
4.	Most of the Aboriginal people live in very bad conditions.	T / F
5.	Some have no work, suffer from diseases, smoke and drink too much.	T / F
6.	Aboriginal people die ten years later than non-Aboriginal people.	T / F
7.	They need better healthcare, better food and education.	T / F
8.	Benan wants to study medicine and help his people one day.	T / F
9.	Today most of the Aboriginal people speak English.	T / F
10.	Benan's favourite hobby is playing football.	T / F
11.	He loves taking photos of Aboriginal people and their lifestyle.	T / F
12.	Benan only paints and draws beautiful motifs.	T / F
13.	He loves drawing old motifs and patterns of rock paintings.	T / F
14.	He is fascinated by their holy mountain Ayers Rock.	T / F
15.	One of his best photos shows a boy with a boomerang and a mobile.	T / F
16.	Benan wants to make an exhibition one day.	T / F

46 Listen to Chloe talking about life in Tehran and **tick the correct answers**:

Track 46

1. They moved to Tehran because
   a. ☐ Chloe's mother is an architect.
   b. ☐ her father was sent there by his firm.
   c. ☐ Chloe attends an international school.
   d. ☐ of the hot weather.

2. What does Chloe not like about her new life?
   a. ☐ The hot weather.
   b. ☐ That her brother has more rights.
   c. ☐ The food.
   d. ☐ Her new school.

3. What is her new dress code?
   a. ☐ The latest fashion.
   b. ☐ Comfortable clothes.
   c. ☐ Long coats and a scarf.
   d. ☐ Blouses with short sleeves.

4. What does she like most about her life in Tehran?
   a. ☐ The beautiful markets.
   b. ☐ The interesting mosques.
   c. ☐ The tiles with their great patterns.
   d. ☐ That it is easy to make new friends.

5. Who does Chloe mostly miss?
   a. ☐ Her mates at school.
   b. ☐ Her teachers.
   c. ☐ Her grandparents.
   d. ☐ Her neighbours.

6. What are Chloe's plans for the future?
   a. ☐ Study architecture.
   b. ☐ Be a female rights activist.

47 Listen to Theo talking about his new neighbour and **circle T** or **F**:

Track 47

1. Theo's new neighbour is an old and very nice man who likes children. T / F
2. The man gave them a list of what they were not allowed to do. T / F
3. They were not allowed to play volleyball or jump into the pond. T / F
4. The cat mustn't climb over the fence and jump into the man's garden. T / F
5. Theo's dad doesn't want to make a barbecue because of the smoke. T / F
6. Theo's mum mustn't invite her friends for an afternoon tea. T / F
7. Theo wants to protest but his parents want a peaceful solution. T / F

48 Listen to the children talking about their school cafeteria and **match the sentence halves:**

Track 48

1. The school cafeteria only serves	a. at their school.
2. Sofia takes her own lunch to school because	b. school lunches.
3. The cafeteria should offer healthy things	c. less meat.
4. There are many vegetarians	d. suggestions.
5. They want to ask the manager for a new	e. unhealthy food.
6. They plan to organise a group for better	f. from various meals.
7. In their lunches there should be	g. make PP presentations.
8. They want to write posters with their	h. she won't buy junk food.
9. In an online poll the pupils can choose	i. and healthier menu.
10. They are going to hand out leaflets and	j. like vegetables and fruits.

49 Listen to the interview about Freddie's protest group and **circle T** or **F:**

Track 49

1. Scarlett is working for the school magazine. T / F
2. Freddie's group is fighting against the kindergarten next to a bar. T / F
3. The guests leave lots of dirt behind. T / F
4. The pavement and the street are full of litter every morning. T / F
5. When he takes his brother to kindergarten they step on broken glass. T / F
6. He founded the group two weeks ago and they have been very active. T / F
7. They handed out leaflets and collected signatures. T / F
8. The owner of the bar invited them for a drink at his bar. T / F
9. 300 pupils went on a protest march in front of the bar. T / F
10. They ask for a closing time of 11 p.m. and more police in this area. T / F

50 Listen to teenagers fighting against cutting down a tree and **circle T** or **F:**

Track 50

1. An old oak tree should be cut down to build a new shopping centre. T / F
2. The tree is more than two hundred years old. T / F
3. People can sit down on five benches around the tree. T / F
4. Kevin is sure that lots of people are going to help them. T / F
5. Lola wants to organise a meeting with their mayor. T / F
6. They want to prepare a list with good arguments. T / F
7. The tree is very important for the fresh air in the town. T / F
8. They want to hand out posters to inform everyone. T / F
9. Kevin wants to go on a protest march and have a sit-in under the tree. T / F
10. They want to inform some TV stations about their project. T / F

51 Listen to Harvey talking about his *Protect the Planet* group and **complete the sentences:**

Track 51

1. They print .... and .... them ....
2. They create .... and write ....
3. They tell people not to .... in the streets.
4. Empty bottles should be taken to ....
5. They tell people to put their old newspapers into .... paper ....
6. Bottles, old newspapers and plastic can be ....
7. People should use shopping bags made of cloth instead of ....
8. On their bikes there is a slogan, "Stay fit and ...."
9. Their parents never drive them short ....
10. They advise people to buy .... food.
11. They organise talks on climate .... , the greenhouse .... and alternative ....
12. They get lots of .... from private people and from firms.

52 Listen to Ruby talking about her personal heroine and **tick the correct answers:**

Track 52

1. Ruby's personal heroine is
   a. ☐ her father's new wife.
   b. ☐ her grandmother.
   c. ☐ her mother.

2. Her father found
   a. ☐ a new wife.
   b. ☐ new children.
   c. ☐ a new dog.

3. Her father sends them
   a. ☐ letters.
   b. ☐ money.
   c. ☐ presents.

4. Her mother never
   a. ☐ cries.
   b. ☐ shouts.
   c. ☐ complains.

5. They sometimes go on a
   a. ☐ camping holiday.
   b. ☐ bike tour.
   c. ☐ safari holiday.

6. Her mother gives them
   a. ☐ many presents.
   b. ☐ a normal family life.
   c. ☐ a lot of money.

7. Her mother is
   a. ☐ angry.
   b. ☐ bad-tempered.
   c. ☐ humorous.

8. Her mum sometimes has
   a. ☐ hard times.
   b. ☐ a black eye.
   c. ☐ no time for Ruby.

53   Listen to the radio programme *Heroes and Heroines* and **circle T** or **F**:

Track 53

1.	The moderator welcomes four guests in the studio.	T / F
2.	The guests are going to talk about their friends.	T / F
3.	There are many reasons why Lucas chose Gandhi as his personal hero.	T / F
4.	Gandhi was peaceful, tolerant and patient.	T / F
5.	He never lied to anybody.	T / F
6.	Gandhi liked pork and beef very much.	T / F
7.	Ella adores Mother Teresa because she lived with poor people.	T / F
8.	Mother Teresa had the feeling that everybody loved her.	T / F
9.	She also cared for ill people and for children that had no parents.	T / F
10.	Mother Teresa received the Nobel Peace Prize in 1989.	T / F
11.	Leo's personal hero is his neighbour.	T / F
12.	His neighbour has to sit in a wheelchair but he is full of hope and joy.	T / F
13.	He lost his arms in an accident.	T / F
14.	His neighbour has got many friends and is interested in everything.	T / F
15.	After the accident he lost his job at the local newspaper.	T / F
16.	With his articles he helped Lucas and his friends.	T / F

54   Listen to the interview with Megan talking about the place she would like to visit and **circle T** or **F**:

Track 54

1.	New Orleans is situated in the South-West of Louisiana.	T / F
2.	The town is the birthplace of soul and reggae.	T / F
3.	Megan doesn't like jazz very much.	T / F
4.	Megan would like to visit the French Quarter.	T / F
5.	In the French Quarter you can see street artists.	T / F
6.	New Orleans is famous for ethnic food.	T / F
7.	The famous French Market is the largest market in the United States.	T / F
8.	In the French Quarter you can find houses from the 18th century.	T / F
9.	Megan knows all those facts because she read a book on New Orleans.	T / F
10.	She'd like to take a ride on the Mississippi River on a steamboat.	T / F
11.	In New Orleans you can also visit a zoo, an aquarium and parks.	T / F
12.	There are lots of festivals in New Orleans.	T / F
13.	In 2015 there was a cyclone in New Orleans.	T / F
14.	The hurricane killed 500 people and flooded 80% of the town.	T / F
15.	The town was rebuilt after the disaster.	T / F
16.	Megan is sure that her dream will come true.	T / F

55 Listen to Molly calling her friend from Vienna and **circle T** or **F**:

Track 55

1.	Molly is in Vienna together with a group of fifteen tourists.	T / F
2.	Her father's parents are too old for the journey.	T / F
3.	The weather is fine with sunshine and 27°C.	T / F
4.	They had a breathtaking view of Vienna from the Giant Ferris Wheel.	T / F
5.	Schönbrunn Castle still is the summer residence of the Habsburgs.	T / F
6.	Molly liked Schönbrunn garden with its fountains and statues.	T / F
7.	They watched the evening exercise of the horses.	T / F
8.	The Hundertwasser House looks wonderful with colours and plants.	T / F
9.	St. Charles's Church is the symbol of Vienna.	T / F
10.	The sight Molly liked most was the Spanish Riding School.	T / F
11.	She found Austrian food very tasty.	T / F
12.	Molly found the exhibition on human bodies very interesting.	T / F
13.	They are going to visit the Danube Tower, the Albertina and Grinzing.	T / F
14.	In the Albertina you can see paintings of Klimt, Schiele and Picasso.	T / F
15.	Her dad wants to take some apple juice back home.	T / F

56 Listen to Ethan talking about his dream holiday and **tick the correct answers:**

Track 56

1. Ethan's dream holiday is
   a. ☐ at the beach.
   b. ☐ reading in the sun.
   c. ☐ in the mountains.
   d. ☐ mountain biking.

2. First, the interviewer thinks that
   a. ☐ it is boring.
   b. ☐ it is very interesting.
   c. ☐ it is too dangerous.
   d. ☐ it is a great adventure.

3. Ethan is going to sleep
   a. ☐ in a hotel.
   b. ☐ in a tent.
   c. ☐ in alpine huts.
   d. ☐ in the grass.

4. His ... are going to join him.
   a. ☐ mum and his sister
   b. ☐ dad and his brother
   c. ☐ cousins
   d. ☐ grandparents

5. For his tour he does NOT need a
   a. ☐ rain jacket.
   b. ☐ helmet and a rope.
   c. ☐ computer game.
   d. ☐ bottle of water.

6. The food he takes with him is
   a. ☐ ice cream.
   b. ☐ yoghurt.
   c. ☐ salad and cakes.
   d. ☐ nuts and dried fruits.

57 Listen to Rose talking about her dream holiday and **circle T** or **F**:

Track 57

1. Rose wants to spend some weeks in the desert. T / F
2. She saw a film with breathtaking landscapes in the desert. T / F
3. She collected pictures of huge yellow and dark red sand dunes. T / F
4. She'd like to take a camel ride at sunset in silvery light. T / F
5. Rose also wants to rent a jeep with four-wheel drive. T / F
6. The heat during the day is not too bad but at night it is very cold. T / F
7. Sandstorms are dangerous but you have time to look for a shelter. T / F
8. Rose says that walking in the sand is very nice. T / F
9. If you lose anything in the sand, you won't find it again. T / F
10. For her, an oasis with palm trees and a little pond is a highlight. T / F

58 Listen to the radio programme *Breakfast All over the world* and **fill in the missing words**:

Track 58

1. Will's favourite breakfast is .... with .... or milk and .... of brown sugar.
2. He also likes .... and eggs with .... mushrooms and ....
3. He also eats fried thin .... with ketchup or Worcester sauce.
4. Before he fries the sausages, he always makes a little .... in the sausages so that they don't ....
5. On Sundays he is .... of baked .... on toast.
6. Will sometimes has black .... with potato ....
7. Elena from Mexico loves tortillas with .... red sauce.
8. The tortillas are filled with .... , ... and eggs.
9. On Sundays she sometimes has a .... cocktail with a very .... sauce.
10. She also likes bacon and eggs with .... and pickled ....
11. She loves to .... sweet cake sticks in thick, hot ....
12. Anila from Delhi only eats .... in the morning like .... , ... , bananas, ... and oranges.
13. Her brother prefers .... in the morning because he needs something ....
14. He also has .... with .... or crispy .... with eggs.
15. He also likes rice with ....

28

59 Listen to the radio programme *Breakfast All over the World* and **tick the correct answers:**

Track 59

1. What does Elsa NOT eat?
   a. ☐ Sandwiches.
   b. ☐ Liver paté.
   c. ☐ Smoked salmon.
   d. ☐ Fresh fruits.

2. What does she put on her bread?
   a. ☐ Nuts.
   b. ☐ Sausages.
   c. ☐ Peppers and cheese.
   d. ☐ Marmalade.

3. What does she have on Sundays?
   a. ☐ A soft boiled egg.
   b. ☐ A milk shake.
   c. ☐ Strawberry jam.
   d. ☐ Chocolate cake.

4. She eats her muesli with
   a. ☐ milk.
   b. ☐ fresh fruits.
   c. ☐ yoghurt and nuts.
   d. ☐ caviar.

5. Pierre dips his croissants in
   a. ☐ orange juice.
   b. ☐ milk.
   c. ☐ hot chocolate.
   d. ☐ coffee with milk.

6. Pierre also loves
   a. ☐ brown bread.
   b. ☐ baguettes with jam.
   c. ☐ dried fruits.
   d. ☐ apple juice.

7. In the summer he sometimes has
   a. ☐ ice cream.
   b. ☐ muesli.
   c. ☐ rice pudding.
   d. ☐ bacon and eggs.

8. Danilo does NOT eat
   a. ☐ tamales.
   b. ☐ rice flour.
   c. ☐ duck eggs.
   d. ☐ banana leaves.

60 Listen to the radio programme *Breakfast All over the World* and **tick the answers that are NOT correct:**

Track 60

1. Husein loves his pancakes with
   a. ☐ butter and honey.
   b. ☐ strawberry jam.
   c. ☐ apricot jam.
   d. ☐ bacon and eggs.

2. At the weekend he has
   a. ☐ goat's cheese.
   b. ☐ cow's cheese.
   c. ☐ dates and oranges.
   d. ☐ black olives.

3. Kai always eats
   a. ☐ soup with beef.
   b. ☐ soup with crab meat.
   c. ☐ soup with chicken.
   d. ☐ soup with pork.

4. Yuna's favourite breakfast is
   a. ☐ fried rice omelette.
   b. ☐ coconut milk rice.
   c. ☐ a multi-grain shake.
   d. ☐ fried sausages.

61 Listen to the radio programme about disasters and **circle T** or **F**:

Track 61

1. Tom and his girlfriend Anna spent their holidays in Portugal.	T / F
2. They rented a bike and drove around.	T / F
3. They enjoyed long walks in eucalyptus woods.	T / F
4. They left the village one day earlier than they had planned.	T / F
5. Tom wanted to enjoy more time at the beach in Faro.	T / F
6. Their parents phoned them because they were worried about the fire.	T / F
7. Big towns were trapped in the flames.	T / F
8. Many people died when they tried to escape the flames.	T / F
9. The heavy storms started the fires.	T / F
10. Fallen trees blocked the roads so the rescue teams were late.	T / F
11. Tom's mum had told him to leave earlier.	T / F

62 Listen to a mountain guide and **circle T** or **F**:

Track 62

1. Nine tourists booked a skiing tour in an off-course area.	T / F
2. The weather was fine but it suddenly changed.	T / F
3. The tourists were afraid and wanted to break the tour off.	T / F
4. The guide got an avalanche warning on his mobile phone.	T / F
5. Seven tourists went down the safe slope with the guide.	T / F
6. The snowfall let up a bit.	T / F
7. The guide saw the avalanche break off the mountain.	T / F
8. He phoned the ambulance at once.	T / F
9. The rescue team looked for the group with dogs and sensors.	T / F
10. Unfortunately, all six skiers were found dead.	T / F

63 Listen to Mr Lopez talking about an earthquake and **circle T** or **F**:

Track 63

1. Mr Lopez hid in the cellar of his house under a door frame.	T / F
2. The shaking lasted for about thirty minutes.	T / F
3. Mr Lopez screamed because he couldn't get out of his prison.	T / F
4. His house had collapsed and he could see the sky above him.	T / F
5. He panicked because smaller earthquakes followed the larger one.	T / F
6. After some hours a search dog brought him something to drink.	T / F
7. He was finally freed and taken to hospital.	T / F
8. His legs and one arm were broken.	T / F
9. His family was safe. They were by the coast during the earthquake.	T / F
10. His son had broken his arm and so the family couldn't return.	T / F

64 Listen to the conversation about Hurricane Maria and **tick the correct answers:**

1. The hurricane had a speed of
   a. ☐ up to 240 km/h.
   b. ☐ up to 260 km/h.
   c. ☐ up to 280 km/h.
   d. ☐ up to 270 km/h.

2. Which sentence is NOT true?
   a. ☐ Roads were flooded.
   b. ☐ Trees were uprooted.
   c. ☐ Roads were blocked.
   d. ☐ Help came quickly.

3. The hurricane blew away
   a. ☐ roofs and cars.
   b. ☐ swimming pools.
   c. ☐ roads.
   d. ☐ caves.

4. Many people died
   a. ☐ in a plane crash.
   b. ☐ under fallen trees.
   c. ☐ from the heat.
   d. ☐ in a forest fire.

5. Roads were blocked by
   a. ☐ cattle.
   b. ☐ a traffic jam.
   c. ☐ mudslides and trees.
   d. ☐ people standing there.

6. Hurricanes intensify because of
   a. ☐ colder oceans.
   b. ☐ mudslides.
   c. ☐ heavy rain.
   d. ☐ climate change.

65 Listen to Ella talking about a TV programme about volcanic eruptions and **fill in the missing words:**

1. The report on TV was about ....
2. Adam .... watches the programme but he was not at home that evening.
3. They showed .... pictures in slow ....
4. A volcano spewed .... and ....
5. The lava was .... down the mountain .... everything.
6. People and cattle could be .... before the ....
7. Small .... could be .... on the Richter scale.
8. Before the outbreak everything was .... and the birds flew away.
9. Then, with an enormous ...., a big cloud of ash and .... was sent into the air.
10. Red .... ran down the mountain.
11. The sun darkened from the volcanic ....

31

66   Listen to the news and **match the sentence halves**:

Track 66

1.	Central Europe has been facing the worst	a.	dams have broken.
2.	The floods have claimed more than	b.	were evacuated.
3.	Cars and tents were washed out into the	c.	were impassable.
4.	Rescue teams, volunteers and soldiers have	d.	of mudslides.
5.	Cities are underwater because	e.	European floods ever.
6.	Before the floods came, people	f.	an economic disaster.
7.	Rivers had to be closed to ships, and roads	g.	ninety victims.
8.	There is also a high danger	h.	tomorrow afternoon.
9.	Tourists have cancelled their trips, which is	i.	sea from a camping site.
10.	The heavy rain will let up towards	j.	been filling sandbags.

67   Listen to a girl trapped in a snowstorm and **tick the correct answers**:

Track 67

1. The girl calls
   a. ☐ the ambulance.
   b. ☐ the Mountain Rescue.
   c. ☐ her parents.
   d. ☐ the fire brigade.

2. The teenagers are trapped in
   a. ☐ a hurricane.
   b. ☐ an avalanche.
   c. ☐ a snowstorm.
   d. ☐ a thunderstorm.

3. The teenagers were on their way
   a. ☐ to Eagle's Peak.
   b. ☐ down the mountain.
   c. ☐ to an alpine hut.
   d. ☐ to Angel's Peak.

4. What should the teens NOT do?
   a. ☐ Huddle together.
   b. ☐ Eat all the food.
   c. ☐ Go back quickly.
   d. ☐ Sing songs.

68   Listen to the interview about the impacts of a drought and **circle T** or **F**:

Track 68

1.	If there is a drought, countries with colder climates are better off.	T / F
2.	In hot regions plants, animals and people suffer a lot in a drought.	T / F
3.	Other consequences of drought may be famine, poverty and death.	T / F
4.	A flood may bring about forest fires.	T / F
5.	The worst impact is that people lose their homes.	T / F
6.	*HAP* means *Hope for African People*.	T / F
7.	In Africa, people drive for miles to find a water hole.	T / F
8.	Carrying water back home is mainly done by the older people.	T / F
9.	Most children go to school regularly.	T / F
10.	To help, we can donate money to volunteer organisations.	T / F

69   Listen to Mrs Harper talking about tsunamis and **circle T** or **F**:

Track 69

1.	A tsunami is an earthquake deep down in the ocean.	T / F
2.	Tsunamis can be up to 30 m high in the open ocean.	T / F
3.	In the open ocean they are small but near the coast they pile up high.	T / F
4.	Tsunamis may be caused by earthquakes deep down in the ocean.	T / F
5.	They may also be caused by volcanic eruptions near the coast.	T / F
6.	When tsunamis hit the coast they destroy everything.	T / F
7.	There are always signs before a tsunami arrives.	T / F
8.	All earthquakes in the ocean create a tsunami.	T / F
9.	One sign is that the water withdraws far away from the coast.	T / F
10.	Sometimes people living on the coast are surprised by a tsunami.	T / F
11.	When the wave hits the coast you have to run away very quickly.	T / F

70   Listen to the interview with Mr Liam Mills, a mountain climber and mountain guide, and **circle T** or **F**:

Track 70

1.	Mr Mills blames the bikers and the tourists for the accidents.	T / F
2.	Tourists often go into the mountains with bad equipment.	T / F
3.	Sometimes you can't make an emergency call in the mountains.	T / F
4.	If the weather is fine you don't have to take warm clothes with you.	T / F
5.	Good shoes, like alpine boots, are a must. Sandals are forbidden.	T / F
6.	You must take water, food and sun cream with you.	T / F
7.	You always have to wear a helmet in the mountains.	T / F
8.	Some accidents happen because people overestimate their abilities.	T / F
9.	Before you start you should get some information on the mountain.	T / F
10.	Somebody should know where you are going in case of an accident.	T / F

71   Listen to Mason talking about survival stories and **circle T** or **F**:

Track 71

1.	Mason loves reading survival stories.	T / F
2.	Robinson Crusoe spends nearly 30 years on a desert island.	T / F
3.	He is the only survivor of the shipwreck.	T / F
4.	He gets weapons and other useful things from the ship before it sinks.	T / F
5.	He lives in a cave, hunts, and grows rice and corn.	T / F
6.	In *Cast Away* Chuck is stranded on an island after a plane crash.	T / F
7.	Mason likes the scene of the rescue a lot.	T / F
8.	Mason would like to go to a survival camp one day.	T / F

72   Listen to the phone-in programme *Speak Out* and **circle T** or **F**:

Track 72

1.	Matilda doesn't want to go on holiday with her parents any longer.	T / F
2.	Her parents like staying at home, sitting in the garden.	T / F
3.	They like to read in the shade under a tree or listen to birds and bees.	T / F
4.	Her parents are into fantasy stories and buy lots of books.	T / F
5.	Matilda wants to do something exciting. She is bored at home.	T / F
6.	Her ideal holiday is swimming, surfing, hiking or climbing.	T / F
7.	Her dilemma is that she fears her parents might be sad about her wish.	T / F
8.	Toby suggests that Matilda should go to a youth camp with her friend.	T / F
9.	Toby was at a youth camp three years ago.	T / F
10.	At the camp Matilda can join in lots of different activities.	T / F

73   Listen to the phone-in programme *Speak Out* and **circle T** or **F**:

Track 73

1.	Amanda's brother is not interested in school any longer.	T / F
2.	He used to be a good pupil and a nice brother.	T / F
3.	In his eyes Amanda is a nerd because she wants to have good marks.	T / F
4.	He likes his sister very much and plays with her a lot.	T / F
5.	Amanda's parents don't want to talk with their son any more.	T / F
6.	When he comes home he smells of cigarettes and alcohol.	T / F
7.	Amanda saw a small bag of marihuana among his school things.	T / F
8.	She doesn't know if she should tell her parents about the small bag.	T / F
9.	The moderator and Mrs Warner tell Amanda not to inform her parents.	T / F

74   Listen to the teenagers' holiday plans and **fill in the missing words**:

Track 74

1. Raymond is going to work at an ....
2. He is .... up for a new mountain bike.
3. Sue's going to spend two weeks at a ....
4. Then she's .... at home for four weeks.
5. They want to try the new .... at the sports centre.
6. Then they are going to .... in Raymond's garden.
7. His father has already bought .... for the house.
8. At the end of August there will be a ....
9. He is going to .... Sue, some friends, and Liam.
10. Sue has .... in the face because she likes Liam a lot.

TAPESCRIPTS, WORDS and KEY

1 Listen to Oliver talking about his favourite singer and **circle** (kreise ein) T (True) or F (False):

Hi, I'm Oliver. I'm 14 and I'd like to tell you some important <u>facts</u> about my <u>favourite</u> singer. Her name is Roberta Morris and she is the best soul singer in the world. She is 28 and black. She was born in New Orleans and is married to the rapper Adam Jones. These days they are living in a villa at Miami Beach. She has got a soft, somewhat <u>rough</u>, but fantastic <u>voice</u>. Her songs are <u>mostly</u> about love and they have wonderful <u>lyrics</u> and a good <u>beat</u>. My brother likes Roberta Morris, too and that's great. We have got <u>the same taste</u> in music. We have all her CDs. We always listen to her music before going to bed.

fact	Tatsache	*mostly*	hauptsächlich
favourite	Lieblings-	*lyrics*	Liedtext(e)
rough	rau	*beat*	Takt / Rhythmus
voice	Stimme	*the same taste*	derselbe Geschmack

1. F (soul singer)
2. T
3. F (New Orleans)
4. F (rapper)
5. F (soft and a bit rough)

6. F (about love)
7. T
8. F (They have got all her CDs.)
9. T
10. F (before going to bed)

2 Listen to the interview with Lionel talking about his favourite song and **tick** (hake an) **the correct answers:**

Interviewer: May I ask you a few questions for our <u>school magazine</u>, Lionel?
Lionel: Yes, of course, <u>go ahead</u>.
Interviewer: <u>Are</u> you <u>into</u> music, Lionel?
Lionel: Yes, I am. Music is very important to me.
Interviewer: What <u>kind</u> of music style do you <u>prefer</u>?
Lionel: I like all kinds of music but at the moment I'm <u>keen on</u> soul. But I never listen to techno or free jazz.
Interviewer: Tell me Lionel, is there any song that is <u>special</u> to you?
Lionel: Yes, there is. The song I like best is "*Never Ever Give Up*" by Ken Mars. The melody and the rhythm are <u>awesome</u> but most of all I love the <u>lyrics</u>. They are excellent.
Interviewer: What is the song about?
Lionel: Ken Mars sings about a boy who was an <u>outsider</u> at school. He had good marks but wasn't very <u>popular with</u> his classmates because he was so clever. His class-mates were really <u>nasty</u> to him <u>except for</u> one girl. She was also <u>bullied</u> because she <u>fancied</u> him. But he didn't give up and <u>made his way up</u> in the world. In the end he became a rich <u>guy</u> and <u>married</u> the girl. After ten years there is a <u>class reunion</u> and he <u>turns out</u> to be the real winner in life. He isn't a loser.
Interviewer: Sounds good.
Lionel: Yes, it <u>definitely</u> is. The lyrics are very <u>comforting</u> to anyone who does not <u>belong with the in-crowd</u>. They <u>mean</u> a lot to me. They show us that <u>it doesn't matter</u> what some classmates think of you and that you should never stop believing in yourself. Ken Mars has an absolutely <u>unique</u> voice. He is able to sing high tones as well as very deep ones.
Interviewer: Is there a special <u>passage</u> that you like best?
Lionel: Yes, most of all I like the refrain: *Never ever give up. Be true to yourself. Everything will turn out fine some day.* This is an important <u>message</u> to every-body. Singing it really makes you feel better if you are down and lonely.
Interviewer: Thank you for talking to me.
Lionel: <u>You're welcome</u>!

school magazine	Schulmagazin	*make one's way up*	seinen Weg machen
go ahead	los / nur zu	*guy*	Kerl
be into	begeistert sein von	*marry*	heiraten
kind	Art	*class reunion*	Klassentreffen
prefer	vorziehen	*turn out*	sich herausstellen
be keen on	stehen auf	*definitely*	zweifellos
special	besonders	*comforting*	tröstlich
awesome	großartig	*belong with the in-crowd*	dazugehören
lyrics	Liedtext(e)	*mean*	bedeuten
outsider	Außenseiter	*it doesn't matter*	es macht nichts aus
popular with	beliebt bei	*unique*	einzigartig
nasty	böse / fies	*voice*	Stimme
except for	außer	*passage*	Stelle / Passage
bullied	tyrannisiert	*message*	Botschaft
fancy	gern mögen	*You're welcome.*	Gern geschehen.

1. a
2. b
3. b
4. c

5. c
6. a
7. b
8. b

3 Listen to Elisa talking about her taste in music and **match** (füge zusammen) **the sentence halves** (die Satzhälften):

As I'm into dancing, I'm highly interested in a good melody and an electrifying beat in a song. The rhythm must be strong and I love long drum solos. Phil Collins does some really great solos and the drummer of the band Santana is fantastic too, not to forget Deep Purple and Chicago. They have all got world-famous drum solos in their songs. I know they are old bands but they are great and skilled. For every song I have got different moves and my friends say that I'm an extremely good dancer. I want to be a professional dancer one day.

be into	begeistert sein von	*forget*	vergessen
highly	höchst	*world-famous*	weltberühmt
electrifying	mitreißend	*skilled*	geschickt / erfahren
beat	Takt / Rhythmus	*move*	Bewegung(-sablauf)
rhythm	Rhythmus	*professional*	Berufs-
drum solo	Trommelsolo		

1. c
2. j
3. e
4. f
5. a

6. b
7. i
8. g
9. d
10. h

4 Listen to Joe talking about music and **circle** (kreise ein) T (True) or F (False):

Well, I haven't got a favourite band or a song I like best. I'm not keen on music videos and I'm not interested in what the stars look like either. I don't listen to songs because of their lyrics because I'm not really interested in a certain message. What I really like in a song is a good rhythm and a strong beat. And what I adore are long guitar solos because I'm a guitar player myself. My favourite guitarist is Mark Knopfler. I think he's the best guitar player in the world. He is able to create strong emotions in his listeners with his guitar. I sometimes listen to techno music, house or jazz. There are some pieces of music that run through my veins and then I become one with the music. In such moments I'm not Joe any more but part of the music. I forget about everything around me. That's what I mainly like about music.

keen on	scharf auf	guitar solo	Gitarrensolo
not ... either	auch nicht	create	schaffen / erzeugen
lyrics	Liedtext(e)	emotion	Gefühl
certain	gewiss	vein	Ader
message	Botschaft	become one with	eins werden mit
rhythm	Rhythmus	part of	ein Teil von
beat	Takt / Rhythmus	mainly	hauptsächlich
adore	sehr gern mögen		

1. F (He hasn't got a favourite song.)
2. F (He isn't keen on music videos and he's not interested in what the stars look like.)
3. F (He is not interested in a certain message.)
4. T
5. T
6. F (not one of the best but the best)
7. T
8. T

5 Listen to the two judges on the TV show *The Next Top Pop Band* and **circle T** (True) or **F** (False):

Judge 1: It's a <u>shame</u> the band didn't even know the <u>lyrics</u>. One girl went on singing "lalala" because she <u>forgot</u> her text.

Judge 2: Yes, but they went on singing <u>at least</u>. What do you think about their <u>moves</u>?

Judge 1: I don't think they can really dance. One <u>guy</u> even <u>stepped</u> on the other guy's toes and went the wrong <u>direction</u>. And one girl <u>bumped into</u> the guy dancing in the middle.

Judge 2: Yes, you're right and their moves looked a bit <u>clumsy</u> and <u>wooden</u>, too. In fact, their moves were boring.

Judge 1: I'm totally with you there. And I <u>fear</u> some members of the band can't sing. I heard some false <u>notes</u>.

Judge 2: I <u>agree</u>. Their music wasn't music, just <u>noise</u>. For me the band didn't <u>sound</u> good. I don't think they found the right song to <u>perform</u>. That song <u>definitely</u> was too difficult for them. There were too many high and deep notes. They don't sing well enough to win any <u>competition</u>.

Judge 1: And I'm of the <u>opinion</u> that a rock band should be dressed in <u>leather</u> and not in green and white <u>suits</u>.

Judge 2: I <u>disagree</u>. I think their outfit was OK, but I can't believe that the <u>audience</u> liked their <u>performance</u>. <u>Still</u>, let's wait until the <u>calls</u> are <u>counted</u>.

Judge 1: Yes, let's wait for the audience to <u>decide</u>.

judge	Preisrichter / Jurymitglied	noise	Lärm
shame	Schande	sound	klingen
lyrics	Liedtext(e)	perform	aufführen
forget, forgot	vergessen, vergaß	definitely	zweifellos
at least	wenigstens	competition	Wettkampf
move	Bewegung	opinion	Meinung
guy	Junge	leather	Leder
step	steigen	suit	Anzug / Kostüm
direction	Richtung	disagree	nicht zustimmen
bump into	anrempeln	audience	Publikum
clumsy	ungeschickt	performance	Aufführung / Darbietung
wooden	hölzern	still	doch
fear	befürchten	call	Anruf
note	Ton / Note	counted	ausgezählt
agree	zustimmen	decide	entscheiden

1. T
2. F (They went on singing.)
3. T
4. F (The boy stepped on a boy's toes.)
5. T
6. T
7. T
8. F (The judge doesn't think so.)
9. F (in green and white suits)
10. F (The judge doesn't think so.)

6   Listen to the two <u>critics</u> on the TV show. **Fill in the words** you hear:

Joe: That was <u>fantastic</u>, Betty! Great! Great! Great!
Claire: Yes, it was a <u>brilliant</u> <u>performance</u>!
Joe: <u>First of all</u>, you look fantastic. You've got <u>what it takes</u>. You look like a star with your <u>curly</u> red hair.
Claire: And you are an excellent singer. You've got a <u>unique</u>, strong <u>voice</u> and you <u>weren't out of tune</u> <u>even</u> in the most difficult <u>sections</u> of the song. And you really <u>chose</u> an <u>extremely</u> difficult song.
Joe: I <u>bet</u> you have been training a lot. You don't need any <u>further</u> training.
Claire: What I find cool is that you don't just stand there while singing but you dance well, too. And the way you shake your hair is really lovely. I <u>agree</u> with Joe that you've got what it takes to be a real superstar.
Joe: Yes, you're going to make it, that's for <u>sure</u>.

critic	Kritiker / -in		*be out of tune*	falsch singen
fantastic	fantastisch		*even*	sogar
brilliant	hervorragend		*section*	Stelle / Teil
performance	Aufführung		*choose, chose*	wählen, wählte
first of all	zu allererst		*extremely*	äußerst
what it takes	was man braucht		*bet*	wetten
curly	lockig		*further*	weiter
unique	einzigartig		*agree*	zustimmen
voice	Stimme		*sure*	sicher

1. That was **fantastic**!
2. It was a **brilliant performance**.
3. You have got **what it takes**.
4. You are an **excellent** singer.

5. You've got a **unique**, strong **voice** and you weren't **out of tune** even in the most **difficult sections**.
6. You chose an **extremely difficult** song.
7. You are going to **make** it, that's for **sure**.

7   Listen to the latest interview with Cathy Clarkson, a pop singer, and **tick** (hake an) the **answers that are NOT correct**:

Interviewer: Hi, Cathy. It's been four years now <u>since</u> you were the winner of the talent show *Mega Star*. How has your life <u>changed</u>?
Cathy: It's changed a lot. Four years ago I wasn't <u>famous</u>. I could go everywhere all alone and nobody knew me. Today I need two bodyguards because <u>otherwise</u> the fans would <u>follow</u> me <u>everywhere</u>. I'm always <u>surrounded</u> by fans.
Interviewer: Yes, that's the <u>price</u> of <u>fame</u>.
Cathy: You're right. <u>You said it</u>.
Interviewer: But you are very <u>successful</u>.
Cathy: Yes, but for my <u>success</u> I have to work very hard. Writing songs, producing a new album, <u>rehearsing</u> every day, going on tour – all that means hard work. But I like it. I'm very <u>ambitious</u>. <u>Moreover</u> I wanted to finish school with good marks. I wanted to have <u>As</u> but without <u>cheating</u>.
Interviewer: How did your <u>classmates</u> <u>react</u> when you won the talent show?
Cathy: It was <u>mixed</u>. Some really helped me because for me there was little time left for studying. They sent me schoolwork and sat with me explaining <u>stuff</u>. <u>On the other hand</u> there were some mates who were <u>awfully</u> <u>jealous</u> and <u>envious</u> of my success and my fame. They said silly things behind my back and <u>spread</u> <u>rumours</u> that were <u>completely</u> <u>untrue</u>. Some were really <u>nasty</u> to me. At the beginning it <u>hurt</u> a lot, but now <u>I'm over it</u>.
Interviewer: What are your plans for the future?
Cathy: First, I'd like to finish my studies at university. I'm studying music but it will still take me some time, as you can <u>surely</u> <u>imagine</u>. I've got to <u>combine</u> my studies and my <u>career</u>. That's a <u>challenge</u>. The only sad thing is that there is no time for a boyfriend right now.

Interviewer:	Yes, <u>that's a pity</u>.
Cathy:	But one day I'd like to have a family. I'd like to get married and have two children.
Interviewer:	Have you got some <u>advice</u> for other winners of talent shows?
Cathy:	Yes, you should follow your hearts. You must love music. You must be ambitious and hard-working. As fame often only <u>lasts</u> for a short <u>period of time</u>, you should never make music only to be famous. Do not <u>long for</u> fame. Then you might end up being <u>disappointed</u> and <u>depressed</u>.
Interviewer:	Thank you for the interview.
Cathy:	It was a <u>pleasure</u>.

since	seit	*jealous*	eifersüchtig
change	verändern	*envious*	neidisch
famous	berühmt	*spread*	verbreiten
otherwise	ansonsten	*rumours*	Gerüchte
follow	folgen	*complete / -ly*	total
everywhere	überall(hin)	*untrue*	falsch / unwahr
surrounded	umgeben von	*nasty*	böse
price	Preis	*hurt*	weh tun
fame	Ruhm	*I'm over it.*	Ich bin darüber hinweg.
You said it.	Sie sagen es.	*sure / -ly*	sicher(lich)
successful	erfolgreich	*imagine*	sich vorstellen
success	Erfolg	*combine*	verbinden
rehearse	proben	*career*	Karriere
ambitious	ehrgeizig	*challenge*	Herausforderung
moreover	darüber hinaus	*That's a pity.*	Das ist schade.
an A	ein Sehr gut	*advice*	Rat
cheat	schwindeln	*last*	dauern
classmate	Klassenkamerad	*period of time*	Zeitspanne
react	reagieren	*long for*	sich sehnen nach
mixed	gemischt	*disappointed*	enttäuscht
stuff	Ding(e)	*depressed*	niedergeschlagen
on the other hand	andererseits	*pleasure*	Vergnügen
awful / -ly	schrecklich		

1.	c		5.	a
2.	a		6.	d
3.	b		7.	d
4.	d		8.	b

8 Listen to Raymond's story and **circle T** (True) or **F** (False):

I was not a <u>superstitious</u> person and I never believed in <u>bad luck</u> until Friday 13ᵗʰ of May last year. Everything that could go wrong went wrong that day, <u>except</u> for one little thing. But let me begin at the beginning.
In the morning I jumped out of bed and fell over Dinah, my cat. I <u>twisted</u> my <u>ankle</u> and <u>limped</u> into the bathroom. <u>Unfortunately</u>, I broke a small <u>mirror</u>. "That <u>means</u> seven years of bad luck!" my little sister said. I got dressed. Then I limped into the kitchen and took my cup of coffee. But it was so hot that I <u>dropped</u> it and <u>spilt</u> the hot coffee over my sweater and my trousers. I had to <u>change my clothes</u>, <u>of course</u>. Then it was really late and I missed my bus to school. As I couldn't walk quickly with my ankle, dad took me to school in his car. On our way a black cat jumped onto the <u>windscreen</u> and dad <u>lost control</u> of the car and <u>crashed</u> into a <u>lamppost</u>. Of course, I was late for school and the teacher was very angry. He was even angrier when I <u>fell asleep</u> during his lesson while he was explaining some grammar. In the break, I <u>bit</u> my tongue while I was eating my sandwich. When I was limping home after school it started raining heavily. At home when I was working at the computer I <u>deleted</u> an important file. That was enough for me! What an awful Friday 13ᵗʰ! I began to cry. I was still crying when somebody rang the doorbell. I <u>wiped</u> my face and opened the door. It was Linda! I <u>fancied</u> her very much but I never <u>dared</u> to ask her out for a date. She wanted to <u>borrow</u> my Maths books. She saw that my eyes were <u>wet</u> and <u>swollen</u> and asked me why I was so sad. I told her about my horrible Friday 13ᵗʰ. Then Linda <u>hugged</u> me! Yes, she really did! I was totally <u>excited</u>! So Friday 13ᵗʰ wasn't that bad after all, was it?

superstitious	abergläubisch	*lose, lost control*	Kontrolle verlieren, verlor die K.
bad luck	Pech	*crash*	krachen
except	außer	*lamppost*	Laternenmast
twist	verdrehen	*fall, fell asleep*	einschlafen, schlief ein
ankle	Knöchel	*bite, bit*	beißen, biss
limp	humpeln	*delete*	löschen
unfortunately	unglücklicherweise	*wipe*	abwischen
mirror	Spiegel	*fancy*	sehr gerne haben
mean	bedeuten	*dare*	wagen
drop, dropped	fallen lassen, ließ fallen	*borrow*	ausborgen
spill, spilt	verschütten, verschüttete	*wet*	nass
change my clothes	mich umziehen	*swollen*	geschwollen
of course	natürlich	*hug, hugged*	umarmen, umarmte
windscreen	Windschutzscheibe	*excited*	aufgeregt

1. F (He wasn't.)
2. T
3. F (his cat)
4. F (he limped)
5. T
6. T
7. T
8. F (his dad)
9. T
10. T
11. F (He bit his tongue.)
12. F (a heavy rain)
13. T
14. T
15. F (He never dared to ask her for a date.)
16. F (Linda hugged Raymond.)

9 Listen to Mr Hall talking about a very strange thing that happened to him and **circle T** (True) or **F** (False):

I wanted to <u>sell</u> my house in Fairwater Street and move to the country. My dream was to buy a farm and <u>grow</u> my own <u>corn</u> and vegetables and have some chickens. But my wife and my children were totally against my plan. Lara, my wife, had a good job in the city and my children didn't want to <u>leave</u> their school and all their friends. We <u>quarrelled</u> a lot about my plans.
One day, when I was on my way home from work it was raining heavily. Suddenly I saw a nice bar in front of me. It was between a baker's and a <u>butcher's</u>. "How <u>strange</u>!" I thought. "I have never seen this bar before!" I <u>decided</u> to have a beer and wait until the rain was over and <u>entered</u> the bar. I didn't know any of the <u>guests</u>. I sat down at the <u>counter</u> and ordered a glass of beer. It <u>tasted</u> <u>delicious</u>! After a while, when I looked out of the window I saw that the sun was shining again. Then, I went home. At the door I was <u>surprised</u> that I couldn't put the key in the <u>lock</u>. I looked at the house again. Yes, it was my house, number 38. Then I had a look at the <u>doorplate</u>. It said "Cunnington" and not "Hall".
I was <u>confused</u> and rang the doorbell. An old woman opened the door. I told her that I was Mr Hall and I lived here in this house number 38. "How strange", she answered. "A family Hall lived here many years ago." "That can't be!" I shouted, "<u>What's the matter</u>? I <u>left</u> home at seven this morning!" I was confused and <u>frightened</u>.
"Do come in," the lady said. "It was a very sad story. Mr Hall sold the house. His wife and his children didn't want to move. His wife fell <u>ill</u> and died of <u>cancer</u> and the children ran away after their mother's <u>death</u>. Nobody saw them again. I can't tell you any more about it. That's all I know." "That's <u>impossible</u>! What <u>shall</u> I do now? I'<u>m caught</u> in the wrong time!" I cried out. "Go back to the bar," the woman said and smiled. "How do you know that I was at a bar?" I asked. But the old lady just smiled and closed the door.
So I ran back to the bar as fast as I could. It was raining again. When I arrived at the place where the bar had been I couldn't find the bar. There was the baker's and the butcher's but there was no bar. I was <u>shaking</u> with <u>fear</u>. Suddenly a car stopped next to me. It was my <u>neighbour</u>. He asked me, "Why are you standing here in the rain <u>staring</u> at the baker's? Can I take you home?" "Yes, thank you, Bill" I answered. I was so happy to see him.
Back home I put the key into the lock. The door <u>sprang</u> open. And in the house my wife and my children were waiting for me to come home for dinner. I can tell you that I was <u>extremely</u> happy. "We are not going to move! We are not going to sell the house!" I shouted and my wife <u>hugged</u> me and the children danced around happily.
Some years later I told them about the strange <u>incident</u>.

40

sell	verkaufen	*What's the matter?*	Was ist los?
grow	anbauen	*leave, left*	verlassen, verließ
corn	Getreide	*be frightened*	sich fürchten
leave	verlassen	*ill*	krank
quarrel	streiten	*cancer*	Krebs
butcher	Fleischhauer	*death*	Tod
strange	seltsam	*impossible*	unmöglich
decide	beschließen	*shall*	sollen
enter	betreten	*be caught*	gefangen sein
guest	Gast	*shake*	zittern
counter	Theke	*fear*	Furcht
taste	schmecken	*neighbour*	Nachbar
delicious	köstlich	*stare*	starren
surprised	erstaunt	*spring, sprang*	springen, sprang
lock	Schloss	*extreme / -ly*	äußerst
doorplate	Türschild	*hug, hugged*	umarmen, umarmte
confused	verwirrt	*incident*	Ereignis

1. F (He wanted to sell it.)
2. F (no cows)
3. T
4. T
5. T
6. F (He didn't know anyone.)
7. T
8. T
9. F (a sad story)
10. T
11. F (to the bar)
12. F (She didn't say anything. She only smiled.)
13. T
14. T
15. T
16. F (He told them about it some years later.)

10 Listen to Liam talking about how he got to know his girlfriend and **tick** (hake an) **the correct options** (Möglichkeiten):

Well, five years ago I was on holiday in Italy with some friends. We had a great time lying at the beach, swimming in the sea and playing beach volleyball. Every afternoon we were playing from five to six. But one day I <u>stepped</u> on something hard in the sand. It <u>hurt</u> and there was blood on the <u>sole</u> of my foot.
A golden earring with a blue stone <u>stuck</u> in my foot. I <u>limped</u> to my room and put a <u>patch</u> on my foot. Then, I went to the <u>receptionist</u> to tell her about the earring. I was waiting at the reception desk when a pretty girl walked up. She was wearing one golden earring with a blue stone in it. I showed her the earring I had found. She was so <u>thankful</u> and happy because the earrings were from her grandmother. She <u>invited</u> me to dinner and that is how we <u>fell in love</u>.

step, stepped	steigen, stieg	*patch*	Pflaster
hurt, hurt	weh tun, tat weh	*receptionist*	Empfangsdame
sole	Sohle	*thankful*	dankbar
stick, stuck	stecken, steckte	*invite*	einladen
limp	hinken	*fall, fell in love*	verlieben, verliebte

1. c
2. c
3. a
4. b
5. b
6. c
7. a
8. a

11 Listen to Rose talking about how she found the man of her dreams and **fill in the missing words:**

I <u>normally</u> do not <u>believe</u> in horoscopes but that morning my brother read out my horoscope to me. It said, "You are going to meet the partner of your dreams today." I went to university and then I did some shopping. In the afternoon I <u>visited</u> <u>a friend of mine</u> <u>in order to</u> <u>pepare</u> for an

important <u>exam</u>. In the evening when I was on my way home, I wanted to <u>cross</u> Elm Street. I waited for the traffic lights to turn to green and <u>stepped</u> onto the <u>pedestrian</u> <u>crossing</u>.
A car <u>jumped the red light</u> and <u>knocked</u> me <u>over</u>. I had a horrible <u>pain</u> in my right foot and arm. The last thing I saw was that there was blood on my new coat. Then I <u>passed out</u>. When I finally <u>came to</u> again, it was ten minutes to midnight. I had my arm and leg <u>in plaster</u> and a <u>bandage</u> around my head.
Suddenly the door to my room opened and a very friendly doctor came in. He explained to me what had happened and told me that I would have to stay in hospital for five weeks. He stayed with me for half an hour and said that if I needed anything, I should ring the bell. He was the <u>doctor in charge</u> for that night. And I'm sure you all can <u>imagine</u> how the story went on! He was the man of my dreams. This time the horoscope didn't <u>lie</u>!

normally	normalerweise	*crossing*	Übergang
believe	glauben	*jump the red light*	bei Rot über die Kreuzung fahren
visit	besuchen	*knock over*	niederstoßen
a friend of mine	mein Freund	*pain*	Schmerz
in order to	um zu	*pass out*	ohnmächtig werden
prepare	vorbereiten	*come to*	zu sich kommen
important	wichtig	*in plaster*	in Gips
exam	Prüfung	*bandage*	Verband
cross	überqueren	*doctor in charge*	diensthabender Arzt
step, stepped	steigen, stieg	*imagine*	vorstellen
pedestrian	Fußgänger	*lie*	lügen

1. Rose normally doesn't **believe** in horoscopes.
2. She went to see a friend in **order** to **prepare** for an exam.
3. She wanted to **cross** a street and stepped onto the pedestrian **crossing**.
4. A car **jumped** the red light and **knocked** her over.
5. She had a horrible **pain** in her **right** foot and arm.
6. There was **blood** on her new **coat**.
7. She passed **out** and when she came **to** again, her arm and her leg were in **plaster** and there was a **bandage** around her head.
8. Just before **midnight**, a **friendly** doctor came into her room.
9. He was the doctor in **charge** for that night.
10. She got to know the man of her **dreams**. So the horoscope didn't lie.

12 Listen to Jonathan talking about the nice coincidence that changed his life and **match** (füge zusammen) **the sentence halves** (die Satzhälften):

My name is Jonathan and I'm going to tell you about the nicest <u>coincidence</u> in my life.
It <u>sometimes</u> happens that a plane is <u>overbooked</u>. And this was the <u>case</u> on my flight to New York three years ago. The <u>airline</u> needed two <u>volunteers</u> who were <u>willing</u> to take a later flight the following day. The airline <u>offered</u> to pay for a five-star hotel for one night and a lovely <u>five-course</u> dinner. As I wasn't in a <u>hurry</u>, I <u>agreed</u> and so did a young lady. We were taken to our hotel by taxi and <u>of course</u> we <u>enjoyed</u> dinner <u>together</u>. It was a romantic <u>candlelight</u> dinner with <u>delicious</u> <u>dishes</u> and excellent wines. We talked a lot and we <u>noticed</u> that we had a lot <u>in common</u>. I wished that the evening would never end. The following day we sat on the plane next to each other and we decided to do all the sightseeing in New York together. And that is how I got to know my wife Emma.

coincidence	Zufall / Fügung	*agree*	zustimmen
sometimes	manchmal	*of course*	natürlich
overbooked	überbucht	*enjoy*	genießen
case	Fall	*together*	gemeinsam
airline	Fluggesellschaft	*candlelight*	bei Kerzenschein
volunteer	Freiwillige(r)	*delicious*	köstlich
be willing	gewillt sein	*dish*	Gericht / Speise
offer	anbieten	*notice*	bemerken
five-course	fünfgängig	*have in common*	gemeinsam haben
hurry	Eile		

1.	j	6.	b
2.	e	7.	a
3.	g	8.	d
4.	i	9.	f
5.	h	10.	c

13 Listen to Jill talking about how she found the boy of her dreams and **tick the correct answers**:

I spent my holidays at a lake together with my cousin Norah. At first I wanted to go hiking in the mountains but then we had a really great time there at the lake. We did a lot of jogging along the lake and spent our afternoons reading in the sun. We didn't talk about problems and we could relax. One day Norah wanted to rent a small boat and row to the other side of the lake. My hands were sliding through the clean water of the lake. Fish were swimming around us and it was nice to watch them. Suddenly I touched something hard. It was a bottle. I tried to grab it and nearly fell into the water. Norah rowed back a bit and finally I managed to get the bottle out of the water. The bottle was closed with a cork and in it there was a sheet of paper. I was curious and pulled the paper out. There was no water in the bottle and the sheet was completely dry. It said, "A lonely heart wants to invite the reader of this letter for a drink at the Candlelight Bar at 8 p.m. on Saturday 12th of July. Bring this bottle with you, please." "That's today!" I said to Norah. "We must go to the bar tonight and find out who the author of this note is." And that was what we did. I was wearing a nice dress with flowers on it and I was holding the bottle in my hands. Of course I was very nervous. Suddenly a young man came up to me and said, "You won the first prize" and he laughed at me in a friendly way. He had nice brown eyes and was very likeable. "And what's the prize?" I asked. "That's me!" he said with a beaming smile.
That was four years ago and next year Fred and I are going to get married.

lake	See	*sheet*	Blatt
hiking	wandern	*curious*	neugierig
mountain	Berg	*lonely*	einsam
along	entlang	*heart*	Herz
relax	sich erholen	*invite*	einladen
rent	mieten	*candlelight*	Kerzenlicht
row	rudern	*author*	Verfasser / Autor
slide	gleiten	*note*	Mitteilung
bottle	Flasche	*of course*	natürlich
grab	ergreifen	*prize*	Preis
nearly	fast / beinahe	*in a friendly way*	freundlich
manage	schaffen	*likeable*	sympathisch
cork	Korken	*beaming*	strahlend

1.	c	3.	a
2.	b	4.	b
		5.	c

14 Listen to the phone-in show and **circle T** (True) or **F** (False):

Interviewer: Welcome to our phone-in show *Angels*. Who is our first caller?
Mary-Ann: It's Mary-Ann from Manchester.
Interviewer: Hello, Mary-Ann. So tell us, please, do you believe in angels?
Mary-Ann: Normally I'm a very realistic person. But what happened to me two months ago made me believe in angels.
Interviewer: Tell us your story.
Mary-Ann: Alright, then. I was on my way to a pop concert when I saw an old woman carrying two heavy bags. She could hardly walk, so I went over to her and asked her if she needed help. She told me that she didn't live far from here and so I took her bags and carried them to her home. She lived in Kensington Garden Road, in

a flat. She invited me for a cup of tea and delicious biscuits. She told me a lot about her life which was very interesting and I forgot about the time. When I finally looked at my watch, it was very late and I hurried to the stadium where the concert would take place. But when I arrived, the entrance was closed and the security didn't let me in. I was so angry. I took the underground and went to see my friend Lucy to tell her about my bad luck. When she opened the door her eyes were full of tears. Then she hugged me and shouted, "Thank goodness! You are alive!" I didn't understand what was going on. She told me that there was a gas explosion near the entrance of the stadium and lots of people who were in the stadium died. I quickly phoned my parents to tell them that I was safe.

Interviewer: Thank you very much for this excellent story, Mary-Ann.

Mary-Ann: But that wasn't the end. The next day I bought flowers. I wanted to visit the old lady because she saved my life. But when I was at the house, there was no old lady on the third floor. And there was no flat number 13. I rang the bell of flat number 12a. A young woman opened the door. I asked her about the old lady. She told me that there were only young families in the house, but many years ago there lived an old lady on the third floor. Her name was Angela Huntington. She died in a gas explosion. So I went to look for her in the local graveyard and put the flowers on her grave to say thank you.

angel	Engel	take place	stattfinden
caller	Anrufer	entrance	Eingang
believe	glauben	bad luck	Pech
normally	normalerweise	tear	Träne
hardly	kaum	hug, hugged	umarmen, umarmte
need	brauchen	thank goodness	Gott sei Dank
far	weit	alive	am Leben
flat	Wohnung	die, died	sterben, starb
invite	einladen	safe	sicher / in Sicherheit
delicious	köstlich	save	retten
biscuit	Keks	local	örtlich
forget, forgot	vergessen, vergaß	graveyard	Friedhof
finally	schließlich	grave	Grab
would	würde		

1. T
2. F (on her way to a pop concert)
3. T
4. F (on the third floor)
5. F (a cup of tea)
6. F (delicious)
7. T
8. T
9. T
10. F (underground)
11. T
12. T
13. T
14. T
15. F (in a gas explosion)
16. T

15 Listen to Jeremy talking about his favourite holidays and **circle T** (True) or **F** (False):

The holiday I liked best was the one at a mountain hut together with my family. It was gorgeous! We could drive up in our car very high but the last bit, about a hundred meters, we had to walk and carry all of our stuff. That's why dad warned us not to take too many things with us.
There were four rooms in the hut. A very small one for me and my brother. There was a bunk bed in it. Then there was one bigger bedroom for my parents, a small bathroom with a basin and a tub and an eat-in kitchen. In this room there was a heavy wooden table and four chairs. There was no electricity and no running water in the hut. We had to fetch the water from a well outside the hut. Then we had to heat the water on the stove to take a bath. For cooking we also had to make a fire in the stove. It was so romantic. We had candles for the evenings because there was no electric light.
Our neighbours were cows and sheep and sometimes deer or rabbits came by. At home I was worried about the fact that our mobile phones wouldn't work in the mountains and that it might be boring without the games I had on my mobile. But it wasn't boring at all. There was so much

to do. For example going down into the woods and <u>collecting</u> <u>mushrooms</u>, <u>picking</u> <u>peppermint</u> to make tea, <u>chopping</u> wood for the stove, walking down to the nearest farm to get meat, eggs, milk, cheese and bread. And there was this lovely cat. We named her Kitty and played with her <u>even if</u> she <u>scratched</u> us. We made paper balls and threw them away and Kitty jumped after them and rolled on the ground like <u>mad</u>. We read a lot because my brother and I are real <u>bookworms</u>. In the evenings we made an open fire in front of the hut and dad took his guitar out and we sang songs. We were all sad when the holidays were over but dad <u>promised</u> we would go there again next year.

mountain hut	Berghütte	*worried*	besorgt
gorgeous	großartig	*fact*	Tatsache
last bit	letztes Stück	*would*	würde
stuff	Dinge	*work*	funktionieren
bunk bed	Stockbett	*boring*	langweilig
basin	Waschbecken	*not ... at all*	überhaupt nicht
tub	Badewanne	*collect*	sammeln
eat-in kitchen	Wohnküche	*mushroom*	Pilz
electricity	Strom	*pick*	pflücken
running water	Fließwasser	*peppermint*	Pfefferminze
fetch	holen	*chop*	hacken
well	Brunnen	*even if*	sogar wenn
heat	erhitzen	*scratch*	kratzen
stove	Ofen	*mad*	verrückt
candle	Kerze	*bookworm*	Bücherwurm
deer	Reh(e)	*promise*	versprechen

1. T
2. T
3. T
4. F (a small room)
5. F (one basin)
6. T
7. T
8. F (no chickens)
9. F (It wasn't boring because they had so much to do.)
10. T
11. F (the nearest farm)
12. F (They played with the cat even if it scratched them.)
13. F (paper balls)
14. F (They read a lot.)
15. T
16. T

16 Listen to the children talking about their holidays and **circle T** (True) or **F** (False):

Emily: Hi, I'm Emily. <u>I'm into</u> mountain climbing. I did a <u>course</u> last year and now I use every free minute to climb <u>rocks</u>. I need a <u>hard hat</u>, a <u>rope</u> and special climbing shoes. I'm really good at climbing. My <u>equipment</u> is <u>expensive</u> but I get some money from my grandparents.

to be into	etwas sehr gerne tun	*rope*	Seil
course	Kurs	*equipment*	Ausrüstung
rock	Felsen	*expensive*	teuer
hard hat	Helm		

Samuel: My name is Samuel. I love sightseeing. I've already been to Paris, Vienna, Rome and London. In <u>each</u> town I visited <u>awesome</u> sights. I saw the Eiffel Tower in Paris, London Eye in London, the Colosseum in Rome and the Prater and Schönbrunn in Vienna. And I love <u>tasting</u> the food in <u>different</u> countries. I've got a large <u>collection</u> of <u>recipes</u> from all over the world. I want to be a cook one day.

each	jede / -r / -s Einzelne	*different*	verschieden
awesome	großartig	*collection*	Sammlung
taste	kosten	*recipe*	Rezept

Laura: Hello, my name is Laura. We always go to Austria for our holidays. In the winters my family and I spend a week in the mountains skiing. Only my brother is a snowboarder. In the summer holidays we love to go camping near a lake. There are lots of beautiful lakes in Austria. Dad loves fishing and <u>rowing</u> a boat. We also go <u>hiking</u> in the mountains and then we always <u>stop for a bite to eat</u> in an <u>alpine hut</u>. We drink milk there and have bread, butter and cheese.

row	rudern	*stop for a bite to eat*	einkehren
hiking	wandern	*alpine hut*	Berghütte

1. T
2. T
3. F (last year)
4. T
5. T

6. F (He wants to be a cook one day.)
7. T
8. T
9. F (They camp near a lake.)
10. T

17 Listen to the interview with Ken about his year in India and **tick** the sentences that do **NOT belong in** (dazugehören) the interview:

Interviewer: Good morning, Ladies and Gentlemen. Today's *Sunday Morning Talk* is with Ken Smith who spent eight months in India.

Ken: Good morning to all you <u>listeners</u> and thank you for having me.

Interviewer: <u>First of all</u>, why did you go to India?

Ken: Well, I have always been <u>interested</u> in that country, in its people, culture and religion. I wanted to <u>get in touch</u> with Indian <u>customs</u>, take photos and <u>taste</u> the Indian food. <u>During</u> my journey I collected about 380 <u>recipes</u> and visited about a hundred temples all over the country.

Interviewer: What was your <u>worst</u> <u>experience</u> during the trip?

Ken: My worst experience was when someone stole all my money out of my <u>sleeping bag</u>. I then had to find work. But it was not too difficult.

Interviewer: What kind of jobs did you do?

Ken: I worked as a <u>shop assistant</u>, then at a British <u>travel agency</u> as a <u>guide</u>. When I had <u>enough</u> money I stopped working and <u>continued</u> my travel. When I <u>ran out of</u> money again, I looked for the next job. I worked as a teacher, a taxi driver, a <u>waiter</u>. I took anything I could get.

Interviewer: Let's talk about the climate in India.

Ken: Well, it was <u>pretty</u> hot in the South. In the north where they <u>grow</u> tea, it was very cold. I worked as a tea leaves <u>picker</u> up there. But <u>gradually</u> I got <u>accustomed</u> to the climate, even to the monsoon rains. Rain like that <u>flooded</u> a town in less than half an hour. Then the water <u>reached</u> up to my knees. Once, after such a monsoon shower my flight was <u>delayed</u> by four hours.

Interviewer: And this <u>leads</u> me to my next question: How did you travel around in India?

Ken: I went by train, plane, bus and on <u>lorries</u>. Once I had to sit on the <u>load area</u> of a lorry. More and more people got onto it. I was sitting among <u>cages</u> with chickens, rabbits and ducks. It was awfully hot. One man had brought half a pig with him and he sat down on it with all those big, black flies around. It was stinking horribly from <u>sweat</u> and blood. After that trip I stopped eating meat. I became a vegetarian. The trip was a horror ride. We went high up a mountain road and before each <u>bend</u> I closed my eyes. If you are <u>afraid of heights</u>, that's not the right trip for you! I <u>managed</u> to <u>survive</u> the <u>scary</u> ride somehow but after it I <u>suffered</u> from a terrible back pain. But the <u>scenery</u> was <u>splendid</u> and <u>stunning</u>.

Interviewer: <u>Unfortunately</u> time is up again. Thank you very much for coming into the studio, Ken. But you will be our <u>guest</u> again in two weeks. Then you are going to give us some information on Indian temples. This was *Sunday Morning Talk*. Bye to all our listeners.

listener	Zuhörer	gradually	allmählich
first of all	zuallererst	accustomed	gewöhnt
interested	interessiert	flood	überfluten
get in touch	in Kontakt kommen	reach	reichen
custom	Brauch	delayed	verspätet
taste	kosten	lead	führen
during	während	lorry	Lastwagen
recipe	Rezept	load area	Ladefläche
worst	schlimmst	cage	Käfig
experience	Erfahrung	sweat	Schweiß
sleeping bag	Schlafsack	bend	Kurve
shop assistant	Verkäufer	afraid of heights	Höhenangst haben
travel agency	Reisebüro	manage	schaffen
guide	Führer	survive	überleben
enough	genug	scary	furchterregend
continue	fortsetzen	suffer	leiden
run out of	nicht mehr haben	scenery	schaffen
waiter	Kellner	splendid	prächtig
pretty	ziemlich	stunning	atemberaubend
grow	anbauen	unfortunately	unglücklicherweise
picker	Pflücker	guest	Gast

Sentences that are not in the interview: **3, 5, 6, 10, 11, 16, 17, 20**

18 Listen to Mrs Robinson talking about the worst holiday in her life and **circle T** (True) or **F** (False):

My worst holiday experience was last year. We have always wanted to spend our holidays at the sea. So we booked a hotel and rented a car for two weeks. During the flight my husband suffered from altitude sickness and he was so happy when we landed. When we arrived, we found out that the hotel was not as nice as was promised in the catalogue. In fact, it was the worst hotel we'd ever been to. We could not move into our room because it was not ready. So while we were waiting for the room to be made, I wanted to go swimming in the pool. Unfortunately there was no water in the pool, only grass and leaves. It took two hours of waiting. Then, finally, our room was ready but you can't imagine how dirty it was! We found cockroaches in the bathroom and there were still long black hairs in our bed. The floor was dusty. My husband took photos of the room as proof. Then we complained to the manager and he promised to do something about it, but he didn't. So I bought new bed linen myself and a broom to sweep the floor. For breakfast we had only bread and some jam but no bacon and eggs, no fruit and the sparkling wine that was promised in the catalogue was never served. The nicest time was when we were at the sea. We read a lot, swam in the warm water and got a very fine tan. We also did some sightseeing in the neighbouring town. On the last day we had an accident. A bus crashed into the back of our car.
My husband was severely injured. He had a broken shoulder and a broken thighbone and had to be taken to hospital. I only had some bruises. But the worst bit was that he couldn't fly back home with me. He had to stay in hospital for five weeks. I will never forget those awful holidays.

worst	schlimmst	proof	Beweis
rent	mieten	complain	sich beschweren
during	während	bed linen	Bettwäsche / Leintuch
altitude sickness	Höhenkrankheit	broom	Besen
not as … as	nicht so … wie	sweep	kehren
promised	versprochen	sparkling wine	Sekt
in fact	tatsächlich	served	serviert
move into	beziehen	tan	Sonnenbräune
unfortunately	unglücklicherweise	neighbouring	benachbart
leaf, leaves	Blatt, Blätter	accident	Unfall
finally	schließlich	crash	krachen
imagine	sich vorstellen	severely injured	schwer verletzt
dirty	schmutzig	thighbone	Oberschenkel(knochen)
cockroach	Kakerlake	bruise	Prellung / Bluterguss
dusty	staubig		

1. T
2. F (her husband)
3. T
4. F (They couldn't move into their room because it wasn't ready.)
5. F (There was no water in the pool.)
6. T
7. F (They complained to the manager.)
8. F (Mrs Robinson cleaned the room herself.)
9. F (no bacon and eggs, no fruit, no sparkling wine)
10. T
11. T
12. F (She and her husband had an accident.)
13. F (A bus crashed into their car.)
14. T
15. T
16. T
17. F (Mrs Robinson had to fly home alone.)

19 Listen to the children talking about a film on dangerous animals and **tick the correct answers:**

Cindy: Last Saturday I went to the cinema with my brother. We wanted to see an interesting film on dangerous animals.

Burt: Sounds good!

Cindy: No, the film was just awful and very scary.

Burt: A scary nature programme?

Cindy: Yes, the scenes were so brutal that I sometimes had to close my eyes. I simply couldn't watch them.

Burt: What kind of scenes were there?

Cindy: Mostly scenes of hunting and eating.

Burt: What animals were in the film?

Cindy: For example, there was a bear that hunted a monkey. The monkey climbed up a tree and screamed like mad. The poor monkey was so scared. But a bear is also a good climber, not as fast as a monkey but it followed the monkey high up in the tree. They climbed higher and higher.

Burt: Did the bear get the monkey?

Cindy: No, fortunately not because the bear was too heavy for a branch. The branch broke and the bear fell down onto the ground.

Burt: Thank heavens! What else was there in the film?

Cindy: There was a snake. That was gross! It swallowed a little pig. Imagine! A little pig!

Burt: Oh no, I'm not sure I will like the film!

Cindy: In another scene there was a crocodile and it bit off the ...

Burt: No, stop it! I don't want to hear any more of it! I am definitely not going to watch this film!

Cindy: I really can't recommend it. But how about watching the nice cartoon *Tiny Grey and his Family*?

Burt: You mean the cute little mouse?

Cindy: Yes, it's the nicest mouse in the world. This would be a fine film for us. It's awesome for children and grown-ups.

Burt: All right. Let's watch it together.

sound	klingen	*else*	noch
awful	schrecklich	*gross*	ekelhaft
scary	furchterregend	*swallow*	schlucken
hunting	das Jagen	*imagine*	sich vorstellen
scream	schreien	*bite, bit*	beißen, biss
mad	verrückt	*definitely*	auf jeden Fall
be scared	sich fürchten	*recommend*	empfehlen
as fast as	so schnell wie	*cute*	niedlich
follow	folgen	*would*	würde
fortunately	glücklicherweise	*awesome*	großartig
branch	Ast	*grown-up*	Erwachsener
thank heavens	Gott sei Dank	*together*	gemeinsam

1. a
2. c
3. c
4. b
5. c
6. a

20 Listen to Helen talking about a film and **match** (füge zusammen) **the sentence halves** (die Satzhälften):

I've seen *Happy Feet*. It's an <u>animated</u> film for children and <u>adults</u>. I went to see it with my parents and my sisters, I <u>mean</u> with the whole family. It is funny and sad <u>at the same time</u>. The little <u>penguins</u> are so <u>cute</u>. Every penguin has to sing his <u>heartsong</u> to find his <u>mate</u>. The story is about a little penguin named Mumble that isn't able to sing but he can <u>tap-dance</u> perfectly. There is a happy ending, <u>of course</u>. But I don't want to <u>give away</u> too much. You should really go and watch it. It's <u>gorgeous</u> and I can <u>warmly</u> <u>recommend</u> it. There are also <u>sequels</u> but I think they aren't as good as the first *Happy Feet*. The first *Happy Feet* is <u>definitely</u> the best.

animated	Zeichentrick-	*tap-dance*	steppen
adult	Erwachsener	*of course*	natürlich
mean	meinen	*give away*	verraten
at the same time	zur selben Zeit	*gorgeous*	großartig
penguin	Pinguin	*warmly*	wärmstens
cute	niedlich	*recommend*	empfehlen
heartsong	Herzenssong	*sequel*	Folge
mate	Partner / -in	*definitely*	auf jeden Fall

| 1. | f | 3. | d | 5. | b | 7. | c |
| 2. | h | 4. | a | 6. | g | 8. | e |

21 Listen to the children talking about dangerous animals in the world and **answer the questions**:

Mark: I think insects are the <u>most dangerous</u> animals in the world.
Brenda: I don't think so. They are so small.
Mark: Yes, but I read about African killer bees. They are very aggressive, they can fly very long <u>distances</u> and they always <u>attack</u> in <u>swarms</u>. Then there is the Tse Tse Fly. The flies are the <u>carriers</u> of very dangerous <u>diseases</u> and up to 250,000 people die from their <u>stings</u> a year. And not to <u>forget</u> the mosquito! I saw a TV programme and it said that a mosquito is the smallest but <u>deadliest</u> animal in the world. A mosquito is even more dangerous than the Tse Tse Fly. Mosquitos carry diseases and kill two to three million people every year.
Brenda: That's awful. But I would<u>n't</u> like to meet a hippo, a rhino or a crocodile <u>either</u>. Hippos and rhinos are <u>highly</u> aggressive and they are fast runners. <u>Moreover</u>, rhinos don't see well and attack everything that moves, even cars.
Mark: Yes, I've heard about that. Did you know that some crocodiles kill their <u>prey</u> with their <u>deadly</u> roll?
Brenda: What's a deadly roll?
Mark: They bite their prey and turn around with it in the water again and again till it <u>drowns</u>.
Brenda: What an awful death! And there are so many <u>venomous</u> animals. Think of the scorpion or the Black Mamba. If you are <u>bitten</u> by a Black Mamba you stop <u>breathing</u> and <u>die</u> <u>within</u> 3 minutes.
Mark: Yes, and there is the Carpet Viper. Its <u>victims</u> <u>bleed to death</u>.
Brenda: We know a lot about deadly animals, don't we? How about giving a short presentation on dangerous animals in our class?
Mark: That's a good idea. This might be interesting for our <u>class mates</u>. I'm going to ask the Biology teacher.

most dangerous	gefährlichst	*prey*	Beute
distance	Entfernung	*deadly*	tödlich
attack	angreifen	*drown*	ertrinken
swarm	Schwarm	*venomous*	giftig
carrier	Übertrager / Träger	*bitten*	gebissen
disease	Krankheit	*breathe*	atmen
sting	Stich	*die*	sterben
forget	vergessen	*within*	innerhalb
deadliest	tödlichst	*victim*	Opfer
not ... either	auch nicht	*bleed to death*	verbluten
highly	höchst	*class mate*	Klassenkamerad
moreover	außerdem		

1. African killer bees are so dangerous because they are very aggressive, they can fly very long distances and they always attack in swarms.
2. They are the carriers of very dangerous diseases. / They carry very dangerous diseases.
3. Hippos and rhinos are highly aggressive and they are fast runners.
4. She tells him that rhinos don't see well and attack everything that moves, even cars.
5. Crocodiles bite their prey and turn around with it in the water again and again till it drowns.
6. If you are bitten by a Black Mamba you stop breathing and die within 3 minutes.
7. Its victims bleed to death.

22 Listen to Grace giving a presentation on the Poison Dart frog and **circle the correct options** (Möglichkeiten):

Today I want to present to you the <u>Poison Dart</u> frog which <u>counts among</u> one of the <u>most dangerous</u> animals in the world. The frogs have enough poison to kill 20,000 mice. They are very colourful. You can find them in orange, blue, black, green and red. Some frogs are <u>brightly</u> coloured in more than one colour with beautiful <u>patterns</u>.
<u>Scientists</u> think that they become so <u>toxic</u> because they <u>feed on poisonous</u> insects, <u>beetles</u> and <u>ants</u>. They <u>capture</u> their <u>prey</u> with their long and <u>sticky</u> tongues. Some people keep the frogs as pets in <u>tanks</u> and feed them insects that are not toxic which <u>ensures</u> that then the frogs aren't poisonous themselves any more. They live in the tropical <u>rainforests</u> of Central and South America. You can find them in trees or under stones and <u>leaves</u>. They are very small, only 20 to 40 millimeters long.
Animals do not eat them because of their bright colours. They may get very old and live from 12 to 20 years. They got their name because <u>hunters</u> needed their poison for their <u>arrows</u>. They <u>rub</u> the arrow <u>tips</u> on the frogs' backs. Their <u>toxin</u> is also used for medicine.
Thank you for your attention and if you have got any questions, just ask me.

poison	Gift	*capture*	fangen
dart	Pfeil	*prey*	Beute
count among	zählen zu	*sticky*	klebrig
most dangerous	gefährlichst	*tank*	Gefäß
brightly	leuchtend	*ensure*	sicherstellen
pattern	Muster	*rainforest*	Regenwald
scientist	Wissenschafter	*leaf, leaves*	Blatt, Blätter
toxic	giftig	*hunter*	Jäger
feed on	sich ernähren von	*arrow*	Pfeil
poisonous	giftig	*rub*	reiben
beetle	Käfer	*tip*	Spitze
ant	Ameise	*toxin*	Gift

1. most
2. 20,000
3. brightly
4. orange, blue, black, green and red
5. Scientists, food
6. poisonous
7. sticky
8. toxic

9. in
10. millimetres
11. do not eat
12. old, 12 to 20 years
13. poison, arrows
14. backs
15. toxin
16. for

23 Listen to Lenny talking about Madame Tussauds in London and **circle T** (True) or **F** (False):

Madame Tussauds is one of the <u>most popular</u> tourist attractions of London. It is a <u>wax</u> museum which shows the wax figures of <u>famous</u> stars like Angelina Jolie, Brad Pitt, Johnny Depp, Leonardo di Caprio, Michael Jackson, Justin Timberlake and many more. It <u>houses</u> for example famous musicians, <u>actors</u>, and <u>politicians</u>. There are also superheroes like Wolverine, Iron Man and Spiderman. You will also find Katniss Everdeen, the <u>main character</u> of the film *The Hunger Games* there, as well as Captain Jack Sparrow and the Terminator. <u>Of course</u>, you can also admire <u>Royal celebrities</u>. The wax figures look so <u>real</u> and you can stand next to your favourites and take photos with them. But you are not allowed to touch the figures.

You should also visit the <u>Chamber</u> of <u>Horrors</u>, but only if you aren't <u>afraid of</u> <u>serial killers</u>, <u>torture</u> and blood. It is not for small children.

Madame Marie Tussaud <u>created</u> her first waxed figure in 1777. Today you can find wax museums all over the world. The museums are also used as <u>settings</u> for <u>scenes</u> in <u>various</u> films.

most popular	berühmtest	chamber	Kammer
wax	Wachs	horror	Schrecken
famous	berühmt	be afraid of	sich fürchten vor
house	beherbergen	serial killer	Serienmörder
actor	Schauspieler	torture	Folter
politician	Politiker	create	schaffen
main character	Hauptcharakter	setting	Filmschauplatz / Kulisse
of course	natürlich	scene	Szene
Royal celebrities	königliche Berühmtheiten	various	verschieden
real	echt		

1. T
2. T
3. T
4. T
5. T
6. T
7. T
8. F (You may take pictures.)
9. F (You are not allowed to touch them.)
10. F (It is not for small children.)
11. T
12. F (1777)
13. T

24 Listen to Teresa talking about Lisbon Oceanarium and **circle T** (True) or **F** (False):

<u>Lisbon</u> Oceanarium is the largest aquarium in Europe. It <u>houses</u> a large <u>collection</u> of fish and birds. But they also <u>display</u> <u>corals</u>, <u>sea snails</u>, <u>jellyfish</u>, frogs in all colours, <u>seals</u>, <u>crabs</u>, <u>sea otters</u>, penguins and plants. In the middle there is a <u>huge</u>, 7 m deep <u>tank</u> for all kinds of <u>sharks</u>, <u>rays</u> and lots more. The <u>main attraction</u> is the large sunfish. It is flat and has got real lips. It looks nice. Around the main tank there are four smaller, <u>separate</u> tanks for fish that sharks <u>might</u> eat if they were <u>together</u> in one tank. But you get the <u>impression</u> that it is only one huge tank. I stayed there for three hours because it was so interesting.

Lisbon	Lissabon	huge	riesig
house	beherbergen	tank	Gefäß
collection	Sammlung	shark	Hai
display	ausstellen / zeigen	ray	Rochen
coral	Koralle	main attraction	Hauptattraktion
sea snail	Meeresschnecke	separate	getrennt
jellyfish	Qualle	might	könnte / würde vielleicht
seal	Seehund	together	gemeinsam
crab	Krabbe	impression	Eindruck
sea otter	Seeotter		

1. F (Europe's)
2. T
3. F (in the middle)
4. T
5. T
6. T
7. F (four tanks)
8. F (You get the impression that it is only one huge tank.)
9. F (Sharks and other fish are in separate tanks.)
10. F (She stayed for three hours because it was so interesting.)

25 Listen to Simon's presentation on the Eiffel Tower and **circle T** (True) or **F** (False):

The Eiffel Tower is <u>named</u> after Gustave Eiffel who <u>constructed</u> the tower. The <u>construction</u> began in January 1887 and the tower was finished in March 1889. Its <u>entire weight</u> is about 10,000 tons. The tower is 324 metres high and has got three <u>levels</u> which are <u>accessible</u> for <u>visitors</u>. There are restaurants on the first and second platforms which are very <u>expensive</u>. There are eight <u>elevators</u> to take you up to the first and second levels. You can also use the <u>stairs</u> but there are more than 600 <u>steps</u> one must climb to the second platform. The tower is brown and must be <u>painted</u> every seven years. The painters need 60 tons of paint. On top of the tower there is a <u>huge</u> radio and TV antenna. If you don't <u>suffer from</u> <u>altitude sickness</u>, you can <u>enjoy</u> the great <u>view</u> of Paris from <u>above</u>. At night the Eiffel Tower is <u>illuminated</u>.

named	benannt	*step*	Stufe
construct	bauen	*painted*	gestrichen
construction	Errichtung	*huge*	riesig
entire weight	Gesamtgewicht	*suffer from*	leiden an
level	Ebene	*altitude sickness*	Höhenkrankheit
accessible	zugänglich	*enjoy*	genießen
visitor	Besucher	*view*	Blick
expensive	teuer	*above*	oben
elevator	Lift	*illuminated*	erleuchtet
stairs	Stiege		

1. T
2. F (1887)
3. F (three levels)
4. T
5. T
6. F (The restaurants are on the first and second platforms.)
7. T
8. T
9. F (every seven years)
10. F (radio and TV antenna)

26 Listen to Sibyl talking about the Globe Theatre and **circle T** (True) or **F** (False):

The Globe Theatre was <u>built</u> in 1599 by the Lord Chamberlain's Men who were <u>actors</u>. Shakespeare played in the same company <u>together</u> with an actor named Richard Burbage. Many of Shakespeare's plays were <u>performed</u> at the Globe Theatre and he played roles in his own plays. <u>Unfortunately</u> the theatre was <u>completely</u> <u>destroyed</u> by a fire during the <u>performance</u> of the play Henry VIII. A <u>cannonball</u> <u>set fire to</u> the house. <u>Luckily</u> nobody was <u>hurt</u> and the theatre was <u>rebuilt</u> one year later. The actors were only men because women were not <u>allowed</u> to play. There was a lot of <u>noise</u> during a performance. People ate, drank, laughed and shouted. About 3000 people watched a play. The <u>audience</u> loved <u>battles</u> and fights on <u>stage</u> and the actors used sheep's blood to make the battle scenes real. The plays were performed only by day because there was no money for <u>candles</u>. When it was raining the audience got <u>wet</u> because there was no <u>roof</u>. It was an open-air theatre. The <u>cheapest</u> places for the audience were next to the stage. The people had to stand there. <u>More expensive</u> places had chairs.
Today's Globe Theatre, called Shakespeare's Globe, is a modern <u>reconstruction</u> of the old theatre. It is not very far from the place where the original theatre was.

built	erbaut	*rebuilt*	wieder erbaut
actor	Schauspieler	*allowed*	erlaubt
together	gemeinsam	*noise*	Lärm
performed	aufgeführt	*audience*	Publikum
unfortunately	unglücklicherweise	*battle*	Schlacht
completely	total	*stage*	Bühne
destroyed	zerstört	*candle*	Kerze
performance	Aufführung	*wet*	nass
cannonball	Kanonenkugel	*roof*	Dach
set fire to	entzünden	*cheapest*	billigst
luckily	glücklicherweise	*more expensive*	teurer
hurt	verletzt	*reconstruction*	Wiederaufbau

1. T
2. T
3. F (A cannonball set fire to the house.)
4. F (Nobody was hurt.)
5. T
6. T
7. F (They only performed in the afternoon because candles were too expensive.)
8. F (It is not very far from the place where the original theatre was.)
9. T
10. F (People had to stand in the cheapest places.)

27 Listen to a <u>tour guide</u> giving a presentation on the Statue of Liberty and **tick the correct options** (Möglichkeiten):

Today I want to give you some important facts on the Statue of Liberty. It is <u>situated</u> on Liberty Island in New York Harbor. It was made from <u>copper</u> by Gustave Eiffel who also <u>constructed</u> the <u>famous</u> Eiffel Tower in Paris. It was a <u>gift</u> from France in 1886. The figure <u>represents</u> the Roman <u>goddess</u> Libertas holding up a <u>torch</u> in her right hand above her head. At her feet you can see a broken <u>chain</u>. The statue is a symbol of <u>freedom</u>. If you are <u>interested in</u> numbers, I'll give you some: The statue is 46 m high. The statue and the <u>pedestal</u> together are 93 m high. The arm holding up the torch is 12.8 m long. Its <u>total weight</u> is 204 tons. <u>Entrance</u> to the statue is free but you have to pay for the <u>ferry</u> which takes you to the island. You have to take the ferry because private boats are not <u>allowed</u>. Only 240 people are allowed to visit the statue a day. <u>Security checks</u> are very <u>strict</u> and you aren't allowed to take anything with you <u>except for</u> a camera and pills you <u>might need</u>. Your bags and <u>umbrellas</u> must be put in lockers. At night the statue is <u>illuminated</u>.

tour guide	Fremdenführer	*pedestal*	Podest
situated	gelegen	*total weight*	Gesamtgewicht
copper	Kupfer	*entrance*	Eintritt
construct	bauen	*ferry*	Fähre
famous	berühmt	*allowed*	erlaubt
gift	Geschenk	*security check*	Sicherheitskontrolle
represent	darstellen	*strict*	streng
goddess	Göttin	*except for*	außer
torch	Fackel	*might need*	vielleicht brauchen
chain	Kette	*umbrella*	Schirm
freedom	Freiheit	*illuminated*	beleuchtet
interested in	interessiert an		

1. a
2. c
3. c
4. b
5. c

6. a
7. b
8. a
9. b

28 Listen to Carla talking about superstition and **circle T** (True) or **F** (False):

Interviewer:	And now we've got a call from Carla. Carla, my first question: Are you a <u>superstitious</u> person?
Carla:	Yes, I am, <u>definitely</u>. I believe in <u>curses</u> and <u>spells</u>.
Interviewer:	Really, do you? You mean that someone puts a spell on you and then you are <u>bewitched</u>?
Carla:	Yes, <u>kind of</u>.
Interviewer:	Can you give us an example?
Carla:	Yes, of course. When I was young I <u>applied</u> for a job in an <u>office</u>. The <u>job interview</u> went fine and I got the job. I was so happy. But then I got to know that there were two brothers who always said <u>nasty</u> things behind my back, things that were <u>completely</u> <u>untrue</u>.
Interviewer:	What kind of <u>rumours</u> did they <u>spread</u>?
Carla:	Well, that I only got the job because of my father's <u>intervention</u>. But my father <u>actually</u> didn't have anything to do with my job. I was <u>awfully</u> <u>hurt</u>. But what hurt me even more was that they told my <u>colleagues</u> they would not be welcome if they liked me or spent time with me. That was <u>pretty</u> awful.
Interviewer:	That was pretty nasty of the men.
Carla:	Yes, it was. But it got even <u>worse</u>. One day I had to go to some <u>further training</u> and <u>guess</u> who I met on the train?
Interviewer:	The two brothers?
Carla:	Exactly! Those three days were <u>hell</u> for me. When I had to do a <u>presentation</u>, they <u>made faces</u> and asked silly questions. They really <u>disturbed</u> me while I was talking

and I began to <u>stammer</u>. They always made fun of me and <u>behaved</u> like <u>mean</u> school <u>bullies</u>. At night I went to sleep crying. And that was why I took <u>revenge</u> and put a spell on them.

Interviewer: What kind of spell?

Carla: I <u>imagined</u> them sitting in a <u>wheelchair</u>. And after some time my curse <u>came true</u>. The older brother <u>suffered</u> a <u>heart attack</u>, the younger one had a bike <u>accident</u>. Both of them ended up in a wheelchair. From then on they couldn't <u>harm</u> anybody any more. Later I wanted to take the curse away from them again, but it didn't work.

Interviewer: So, to all our listeners, be careful about curses! And Carla, thank you for your interesting and <u>frightening</u> story.

superstitious	abergläubisch	worse	schlimmer
definitely	auf jeden Fall	further training	Fortbildung
curse	Fluch	guess	raten
spell	Zauber	hell	Hölle
bewitched	verhext	presentation	Präsentation
kind of	so ungefähr	make faces	Grimassen schneiden
apply	sich bewerben	disturb	stören
office	Büro	stammer	stottern / stammeln
job interview	Bewerbungsgespräch	behave	sich benehmen
nasty	schlimm	mean	gemein
completely	total	bully	Tyrann
untrue	unwahr	revenge	Rache
rumour	Gerücht	imagine	sich vorstellen
spread	verbreiten	wheelchair	Rollstuhl
intervention	Vermittlung / Einmischung	come true	wahr werden
actually	tatsächlich	suffer	erleiden
awfully	schrecklich	heart attack	Herzanfall
hurt	verletzt	accident	Unfall
colleague	Kollege	harm	Schaden zufügen
pretty	ziemlich	frightening	beängstigend

1. T
2. T
3. F (They didn't help her. They bullied her.)
4. T
5. T
6. F (It was hell for her.)
7. T
8. T
9. T
10. F (It came true.)
11. F (the older brother)
12. F (The older brother suffered a heart attack.)

29 Listen to the interview with Tran Duc Thien about superstition in Vietnam and **circle T** (True) or **F** (False):

Moderator: This evening we <u>welcome</u> Mr Tran Duc Thien <u>born</u> in Vietnam who is going to talk to us about <u>superstition</u> in Vietnam.

Thien: Thank you for having me. Well, Vietnamese <u>people</u> are very superstitious.

Moderator: Can you give us some examples?

Thien: Well, when a baby is born we never <u>express</u> <u>admiration</u> for the <u>new-born</u> child because then the <u>devils</u> <u>might</u> get <u>interested</u> in the child and take the baby away. So a mother would call her <u>handsome</u> son for example "my dear <u>ugly</u> baby". So every child gets two names: a bad one and a good one, but at home we call our <u>family members</u> only by their bad names. Some mothers even <u>dress</u> their boys as girls and give them girls' names.

Moderator: That's interesting. Why is that?

Thien: That's because devils and <u>evil spirits</u> are more interested in boys than in girls. You will often find <u>mirrors</u> on <u>front doors</u> because we <u>believe</u> that a <u>dragon</u> who wants to <u>enter</u> the house will see his own <u>reflection</u> in the mirror. Then the dragon will go away because he is <u>sure</u> that another dragon lives in the house.

Moderator: How <u>amazing</u>! Tell us more!

Thien: Vietnamese <u>housewives</u> always put <u>at least</u> two <u>bowls</u> of rice on a table. One portion of rice is for the dead family members. We also give presents made of paper to them. Our dead relatives need the same things in their afterlife as we need on earth. And that is why we burn paper houses, bicycles, refrigerators, motorbikes, fake money and so on. If we burn the things, the smoke will take the things away to them.

Moderator: How do you celebrate the New Year?

Thien: We call it Tet and the festival lasts up to nine days. All houses are decorated with flowers and paper lanterns. We visit our relatives. Tet also means family gatherings to us. We wish good luck to our family and friends. We wish good health and lots of money. We also give some lucky money wrapped in red paper to the children when we visit someone. Then we make a lot of noise. We clap pots and pans together to scare the evil ghosts away. And food, of course is extremely important, too. My favourite food is sticky rice cake filled with beans or meat. We wrap the cake in leaves. And buying a bag of salt means good luck too. But there are many things we must avoid at Tet. For example, breaking a glass or saying unlucky words.

Moderator: What are unlucky words?

Thien: Unlucky words are "sad, die, unhappy, ill, evil" and so on. We must not wear the colours black and white but lucky colours like red or pink. Housewives must not sweep the floor because then they sweep all the good luck out of the house. Last but not least we ask fortune tellers for our future. And there is something else that is very important: On the first day of the New Year we hope for the first visitor to be a happy, wealthy and healthy person. Sometimes we even invite such a lucky person to be the first visitor to knock at our house.

Moderator: There are still so many interesting things to ask you about your culture but I'm afraid time is up.

Thien: Yes, I could go on talking for hours and hours. But thank you very much for inviting me.

Moderator: You're welcome.

welcome	begrüßen	burn	verbrennen
born	geboren	refrigerator	Kühlschrank
superstition	Aberglaube	fake	unecht / falsch
people	Leute / Volk	smoke	Rauch
express	ausdrücken	celebrate	feiern
admiration	Bewunderung	last	dauern
new-born	neugeboren	decorated	geschmückt
devil	Teufel	lantern	Laterne
might	könnte vielleicht	mean	bedeuten
interested	interessiert	gathering	Treffen / Zusammenkunft
handsome	hübsch	health	Gesundheit
ugly	hässlich	wrapped	eingewickelt
family member	Familienmitglied	visit	besuchen
dress	anziehen	noise	Lärm
evil spirit	böser Geist	clap	schlagen / klatschen
mirror	Spiegel	pot	Topf
front door	Haustür	pan	Pfanne
believe	glauben	scare away	verjagen
dragon	Drache	ghost	Geist
enter	hineingehen	extremely	äußerst
reflection	Spiegelbild	sticky	klebrig
sure	sicher	leaf, leaves	Blatt, Blätter
amazing	erstaunlich	avoid	vermeiden
housewife	Hausfrau	sweep	kehren
at least	mindestens	last but not least	nicht zuletzt
bowl	Schüssel	fortune teller	Wahrsager
portion	Portion	else	noch
dead	tot	visitor	Besucher
made of paper	aus Papier gemacht	wealthy	wohlhabend
relative	Verwandter	invite	einladen
same	gleich	be afraid	befürchten
afterlife	Leben nach dem Tod	You're welcome.	Gern geschehen.

1. F (They never express admiration because they fear that devils might get interested in the child.)
2. T
3. T
4. T
5. F (They are more interested in boys.)
6. F (on the front door against dragons)
7. T
8. F (for the dead family members) T
9. F (They only burn paper things for them.)
10. T
11. F (for up to nine days)
12. T
13. T
14. T
15. F (filled with beans or meat)
16. T
17. F (They mustn't say unlucky words.)
18. F (They mustn't clean the floor because they might sweep the good luck out of the house.)
19. T
20. T

30 Listen to the phone-in show *Ask Everybody* and **fill in the missing words:**

Mandy: Hi, everybody! This is Mandy. I've got a real problem with my best friend. Last weekend we <u>fell out</u> at a disco because she danced with my boyfriend and she <u>even</u> kissed him right in front of me. I didn't say a word. I just <u>stared</u> at them and then I went away. I <u>am finished with</u> <u>both</u> of them and now I don't even answer their calls. What would you do if you were <u>in my place</u>?

Moderator: Thank you Mandy for telling us your problem. And here's our first <u>caller</u>. Tell us who you are.

Thomas: Hi, my name's Thomas. Mandy, I would have done <u>the same</u>. It was good that you didn't shout at them or cry, so you <u>saved face</u>. Try not to be too sad. But both of them do not <u>deserve</u> your <u>friendship</u>. A true best friend doesn't kiss your boyfriend. That's an absolute <u>No-Go</u>!

Moderator: Thank you, Thomas. And who is next <u>on the line</u>?

Olivia: Hi, I'm Olivia. I wouldn't have gone away without saying anything. It was <u>perhaps</u> only one <u>harmless</u> kiss. Perhaps your best friend drank one glass too much. Don't be so <u>unforgiving</u>. My <u>advice</u>: Call them and talk to them again.

Moderator: Thank you Olivia. And next is Boris. Now, what advice would you like to give to Mandy?

Boris: Hi, Mandy. There is only one <u>solution</u> to the problem: look for another best friend and another boyfriend. Drinking too much is no <u>excuse</u> for me! You deserve better! Even if you forgave them, this kiss would stand between you and them <u>forever</u>. And that's not a good basis for an <u>honest</u> <u>relationship</u>.

Moderator: Thank you for calling. And time is up again. Meet us again next week!

fall out	zerstreiten	*No-Go*	Handlung, die nicht passt
even	sogar	*on the line*	in der Leitung
stare	starren	*perhaps*	vielleicht
to be finished with	Freundschaft beendet haben	*harmless*	harmlos
both	beide	*unforgiving*	nachtragend
in my place	an meiner Stelle	*advice*	Rat
caller	Anrufer	*solution*	Lösung
the same	dasselbe	*excuse*	Entschuldigung
save face	sein Gesicht wahren	*forever*	für immer
deserve	verdienen	*honest*	ehrlich
friendship	Freundschaft	*relationship*	Beziehung

1. I have got a real **problem** with my best friend.
2. Last weekend we **fell out** at a disco.
3. She kissed my **boyfriend** right in **front** of me.
4. I **am finished** with both of them.
5. I don't **answer** their **calls**.
6. Here is our first **caller**.
7. I would have done the **same**.
8. They don't deserve your **friendship**.
9. Don't be so **unforgiving**.
10. What **advice** would you like to give to Mandy?
11. There is only one **solution** to the problem.
12. That's not a good basis for an honest **relationship**.

31 Listen to the phone-in radio programme and **circle T** (True) or **F** (False):

Moderator:	Hello, this is *Frank's Call-In Show*. Our <u>topic</u> for today is: true friends. And who is our first <u>caller</u>?
Fiona:	It's Fiona.
Moderator:	Hi, Fiona. Tell us what a true friend <u>means</u> to you.
Fiona:	Well, for me a true friend is someone I can <u>trust</u> and who <u>stands by me</u> in hard times. He or she should be <u>honest</u> and a real friend shouldn't <u>even</u> tell me <u>white lies</u>.
Moderator:	What do you <u>mean</u> by white lies?
Fiona:	For example, if I wear a dress that doesn't <u>suit</u> me at all, my best friend should tell me <u>frankly</u> that I can't wear that dress.
Moderator:	Oh yes, I see. What <u>else</u> do you look for in a friend?
Fiona:	For me, a friend should be <u>reliable</u> and <u>understanding</u> and most important is that a friend listens to you if you have got a problem. I think these are the <u>essential</u> things for a good <u>friendship</u>.
Moderator:	Thank you for calling, Fiona. Our next caller is Simon. Hi, Simon. What do you look for in a friend?
Simon:	We must have fun together and <u>share</u> the same <u>interests</u>. We should <u>spend</u> a lot of time together. And a good friend <u>definitely</u> must keep a <u>secret</u> and not tell everybody. Yes, a good friend should be <u>discreet</u> and of course he should understand my problems. My best friend should be a sporty person because <u>I'm into</u> sports. He should be a good skier and he should <u>be fond of</u> riding his bike. He should <u>be able to</u> swim and climb mountains. He should <u>be keen on</u> playing volleyball. He should like to try something new. Yes, that's exactly what I look for in a friend.
Moderator:	Thank you, Simon. Next is Clarissa. What about you, Clarissa? Which <u>qualities</u> do you look for in a friend?
Clarissa:	It's important in a friend that he or she is <u>helpful</u> and they should <u>comfort</u> me when I'm down. For me, a friend must be <u>kind</u> and <u>caring</u> and he or she must stand by me when I need someone to talk to. I think it's <u>essential</u> that a friend isn't <u>jealous</u> because <u>jealousy</u> is a <u>sign</u> of <u>mistrust</u> and mistrust has no place in a true friendship. <u>Moreover</u>, my friend should <u>hug</u> me when I feel <u>depressed</u>. These are the most important qualities I look for in a friend.
Moderator:	Thank you for calling Clarissa. And time is up again. Meet me again at *Frank's Call-In Show* at five o'clock on Friday next week. Thank you for listening and good bye.

topic	Thema	*secret*	Geheimnis
caller	Anrufer	*discreet*	diskret
mean	bedeuten	*be into*	etwas sehr gerne tun
trust	vertrauen	*be fond of*	etwas sehr gerne mögen
stand by me	mir zur Seite stehen / zu mir stehen	*be able to*	fähig sein / können
honest	ehrlich	*be keen on*	etwas sehr gerne tun
even	sogar	*quality*	Eigenschaft
white lie	Notlüge	*helpful*	hilfsbereit
mean	meinen	*comfort*	trösten
suit	passen	*kind*	freundlich
frankly	offen	*caring*	fürsorglich / liebevoll
else	noch	*essential*	wichtig
reliable	verlässlich	*jealous*	eifersüchtig
understanding	verständnisvoll	*jealousy*	Eifersucht
essential	wichtig	*sign*	Zeichen
friendship	Freundschaft	*mistrust*	Misstrauen
share	teilen	*moreover*	außerdem
interest	Interesse	*hug*	umarmen
spend	verbringen	*depressed*	deprimiert
definitely	auf jeden Fall		

1. T
2. T
3. F (He even shouldn't tell her white lies.)
4. T
5. T
6. F (It is important that a friend listens to you.)

7.	T	14.	F (climb mountains)
8.	T	15.	T
9.	F (They should spend a lot of time together.)	16.	T
10.	T	17.	F (caring)
11.	T	18.	T
12.	F (He should be a good skier and be fond of riding his bike.)	19.	T
13.	F (playing volleyball)	20.	F (hug)

32 Listen to Adrian and Sally talking about <u>friendship</u> and **tick** (hake an) **the answers that are NOT correct:**

Adrian: For me it is a must that my friend doesn't get himself into <u>trouble</u> by drinking or taking <u>drugs</u>. My friend must be <u>reasonable</u> and <u>reliable</u>. He should be fit, like sports and <u>of course</u>, he should be a non-smoker. He should be fair and after a <u>quarrel</u> we should <u>be ready to</u> <u>apologize</u>. He should keep our <u>secrets</u> and not tell everybody. <u>By the way</u>, the best way to have a good friend is to be a good friend yourself.

Sally: You are right, Adrian. I'd like to <u>add</u> that you have only a few really good friends. Sometimes you only have one. Look at all those friends on Facebook, for example. You call them "friends" but they are never best friends. They are just people you <u>hang out with</u> or <u>share</u> some photos or <u>messages</u> with and you don't even know most of them. So, I would call them "contacts". Real friends make it <u>easier</u> for you to live. They help you to be a little better. They give you <u>confidence</u> and <u>support</u>. They <u>cheer</u> you <u>on</u> when you are down and are not <u>jealous</u> when you have <u>achieved</u> something great. They share your happiness, <u>congratulate</u> you and <u>encourage</u> you. They try not to <u>hurt</u> your <u>feelings</u> and if they <u>happen to</u> hurt you, they apologize. You <u>simply</u> feel good in their <u>company</u>. Yes, that's my <u>opinion</u> on friendship.

friendship	Freundschaft	*easier*	leichter
trouble	Schwierigkeit	*confidence*	Selbstvertrauen
drug	Droge	*support*	Unterstützung
reasonable	vernünftig	*cheer on*	anspornen
reliable	verlässlich	*jealous*	eifersüchtig
of course	natürlich	*achieve*	erreichen
quarrel	Streit	*congratulate*	gratulieren
be ready to	bereit sein zu	*encourage*	aufmuntern
apologize	sich entschuldigen	*hurt*	verletzen
secret	Geheimnis	*feeling*	Gefühl
by the way	übrigens	*happen to do*	zufällig etwas tun
add	hinzufügen	*simply*	einfach
hang out with	herumhängen mit	*company*	Gesellschaft
share	teilen	*opinion*	Meinung
message	Botschaft		

1.	c	5.	b, c, d (For Sally these are only contacts, no real friends.)
2.	d		
3.	a	6.	a
4.	b		

33 Listen to Lauren giving her opinion on what a best friend means to her and **fill in the missing words:**

<u>First of all</u>, my best friend should be a girl. She should be <u>trustworthy</u>, should be able to talk to me about everything and should <u>stand up for</u> me. For me, a good friend <u>means</u> being <u>helpful</u> and <u>supportive</u>. She should be <u>open-minded</u> and <u>take care of</u> me. A good friend does everything for me and with me, even <u>silly</u> things. My best friend should be someone I can have fun with and she should <u>make me laugh</u> even if I'm sad. A real friend knows me well. She knows all about my <u>weaknesses</u>. She always tells the <u>truth</u> even if it's not the things I want to hear. With a good friend I can be myself without having to <u>pretend</u> to be <u>somebody else</u>. We should like

similar things and have <u>the same interests</u> like, for example, travelling, sports or going shopping. My best friend should <u>be into</u> horses because I'm <u>fond of</u> horses too and she should be very good at riding. Yes, that's my <u>idea</u> of a perfect <u>friendship</u>.

first of all	zuallererst	*weakness*	Schwäche
trustworthy	zuverlässig	*truth*	Wahrheit
stand up for	sich einsetzen für	*pretend*	so tun als ob
mean	bedeuten	*somebody else*	jemand anderer
helpful	hilfsbereit	*similar*	ähnlich
supportive	unterstützend	*the same interests*	die gleichen Interessen
open-minded	vorurteilsfrei / aufgeschlossen	*be into*	etwas sehr gerne tun
take care of	sich kümmern um	*be fond of*	etwas sehr mögen
silly	dumm	*idea*	Idee
make me laugh	mich zum Lachen bringen	*friendship*	Freundschaft

1. Lauren's best friend should **stand up** for her.
2. She should be **helpful** and supportive.
3. She should be open-minded and take **care** of her.
4. A good friend should do **everything** for her and with her.
5. They should have **fun** together and she should make her **laugh**.
6. A real friend always tells the **truth**.
7. She can be herself without having to **pretend** to be somebody else.
8. They should like **similar** things and have the **same** interests.
9. Her best friend should be **into** horses and she should be **good at riding**.
10. That's her **idea** of a perfect **friendship**.

34 Listen to the telephone call between two friends and **circle T** (true) or **F** (false):

Robert: Hi, April. <u>Guess what</u>! I'm going to have a <u>tattoo</u> on my arm! A big, black spider!
April: What, a tattoo? Are you crazy, Robert? You can't do that! Have you asked your parents yet?
Robert: No, I haven't <u>so far</u> because if I ask them, they will say "no".
April: <u>Of course</u> they will! If you have a spider tattooed on your arm, you will look <u>awful</u>! I <u>promise</u>! I'm <u>dead against</u> tattoos. They <u>destroy</u> your <u>skin</u>. The <u>needle</u> <u>hurts</u> badly. <u>Moreover</u>, you might get an <u>infection</u> and your tattoo will never <u>come off</u> again.
Robert: When I'm <u>grown-up</u> I can go and see a doctor to <u>remove</u> it.
April: That means <u>pain</u> for you again and it's <u>expensive</u>. If you have that terrible tattoo, I think Amanda will <u>break up</u> with you.
Robert: No, she will <u>definitely</u> like it. I've known her since <u>primary school</u> and I'm sure, she won't <u>fall out with</u> me. You are just <u>jealous</u>!
April: Me, jealous? You're <u>nuts</u>! Amanda is <u>a friend of mine</u>! You know that I like her very much.
Robert: <u>By the way</u>, I don't need your <u>advice</u>. Please <u>mind</u> your <u>own business</u>. I thought you were my friend.
April: Robert, I'm talking to you as a real friend, <u>honestly</u>. I don't think you will look cool with a tattoo. We have known <u>each other</u> since we were little kids, haven't we? We were in the same group in kindergarten. Have I ever <u>lied</u> to you? I have <u>kept</u> all our <u>secrets</u>. I have never <u>interfered with</u> your life.
We have always <u>got on well with</u> each other. I don't want to have an <u>argument</u> with you. All I'm doing now is trying to be honest with you. Don't <u>sulk</u> but ask your mum for advice. By the way, how about an earring <u>instead of</u> the tattoo? Earrings are cool and you can take them out again.
Robert: I don't want to discuss it with you any longer. But OK, I'll think about it. See you at school tomorrow. And don't tell anybody about it. <u>Promise</u>?
April: Promise! We are still best friends <u>after all</u>, <u>aren't we</u>?
Robert: Yes, of course we are.
April: See you tomorrow.

Guess what!	Rate mal!	*fall out with*	nicht mehr sprechen mit
tattoo	Tätowierung	*jealous*	eifersüchtig
so far	bis jetzt	*be nuts*	verrückt sein
of course	natürlich	*a friend of mine*	ein Freund von mir
awful	schrecklich	*by the way*	übrigens
promise	versprechen	*advice*	Rat
dead against	total dagegen	*mind*	sich kümmern um
destroy	zerstören	*own business*	eigene Angelegenheit
skin	Haut	*honestly*	ehrlich
needle	Nadel	*each other*	einander
hurt	wehtun	*lie, lied*	lügen, log
moreover	außerdem	*keep, kept*	bewahren, bewahrte
infection	Infektion	*secret*	Geheimnis
come off	weggehen	*interfere with*	sich einmischen in
grown-up	erwachsen	*get on well with*	gut auskommen mit
remove	entfernen	*argument*	Streit
pain	Schmerz	*sulk*	schmollen
expensive	teuer	*instead of*	anstelle von
break up	Beziehung beenden	*promise*	versprechen
definitely	sicherlich	*after all*	nach allem / schließlich
primary school	Volksschule	*aren't we?*	nicht wahr?

1. F (a spider)
2. T
3. F (He hasn't asked them yet.)
4. T
5. T
6. T
7. T

8. F (No, she isn't. She likes her very much.)
9. F (He is angry and says that he doesn't need her advice.)
10. T
11. T
12. T
13. T

35 Listen to the telephone conversation and **tick the correct answers:**

Agony Aunt:	And who is next <u>on the line</u>?
Lara:	It's Lara.
Agony Aunt:	Hi Lara. How can I help you? Tell me your problem.
Lara:	Well, there is Ann. She is a new girl in our class. I tried to be nice to her because she didn't know anybody. I showed her our school building, took her to the <u>library</u>, <u>invited</u> her to my house and <u>introduced</u> her to some of my friends. But now she invites all the others <u>except for</u> me. She had a garden party without telling me. They met at the ice cream <u>parlour</u> and she paid for the ice cream and they went to the cinema and she paid again for the tickets but nobody told me about the <u>meeting</u>. And there <u>was</u> such a nice film <u>on</u>! She <u>even</u> bought the same pink jeans as me. <u>Fortunately</u>, she couldn't buy the same pink pullover because I bought the last one. And now she even wears the same <u>haircut</u> as me. Yesterday I spoke to Sandy, one of my friends, and asked her why they didn't tell me about the ice cream parlour and the cinema.
Agony Aunt:	That was a good idea. What did Sandy say?
Lara:	She told me that Ann said I didn't have time and wanted to <u>be left alone</u>. I was so <u>furious</u>.
Agony Aunt:	I can <u>imagine</u> that!
Lara:	Why did she do that?
Agony Aunt:	<u>Perhaps</u> she just wants to be like you. She <u>envies</u> you because you have got lots of nice friends. Another <u>possible</u> <u>reason</u> <u>might</u> be that she is <u>jealous</u> of you. <u>Anyway</u>, Ann has got a real problem.
Lara:	I <u>fear</u> she wants to take my friends away from me.
Agony Aunt:	Yes, it <u>seems</u> so. She wants to buy your friends with ice cream and cinema tickets. You <u>definitely</u> have to do something about it. My <u>advice</u> is that you should tell your friends the <u>truth</u> about Ann. Tell them that Ann <u>lied</u> to them and did not ask you to come with them. You have known your friends for years now and they know you well. I'm <u>sure</u> you can <u>sort out</u> this problem. And you have to talk to

Lara:		Ann as well.	
		But I don't want to talk to Ann any more.	
Agony Aunt:		<u>Sulking</u> or being <u>mean</u> to Ann are not the best solutions, Lara. You should talk to Ann when the other girls are there too. Then, she must <u>confess</u> and explain why she did that to you.	
Lara:		Yes, I will. Thank you for listening to me.	
Agony Aunt:		You're welcome.	

on the line	in der Leitung	*possible*	möglich
library	Bücherei	*reason*	Grund
invite	einladen	*might*	könnte vielleicht
introduce	vorstellen	*jealous*	eifersüchtig
except for	außer	*anyway*	wie auch immer
parlour	Salon	*fear*	befürchten
meeting	Treffen	*seem*	scheinen
to be on	gespielt werden	*definitely*	auf jeden Fall
even	sogar	*advice*	Rat
fortunately	glücklicherweise	*truth*	Wahrheit
haircut	Haarschnitt	*lie*	lügen
be left alone	in Ruhe gelassen werden	*sure*	sicher
furious	wütend	*sort out*	klären / regeln
imagine	sich vorstellen	*sulk*	schmollen
perhaps	vielleicht	*mean*	böse / gemein
envy	beneiden	*confess*	zugeben

1. a
2. b
3. d

4. c
5. a
6. d

36 Listen to Kim and Carrie who are best friends and **circle T** (True) or **F** (False):

Moderator: And here in our studio we <u>welcome</u> Kim and Carrie. You <u>look like</u> <u>twins</u> but you aren't.
Kim: Exactly. We aren'<u>t even</u> sisters. We're just best friends.
Moderator: For how long have you known each other?
Carrie: For seven years now. We went to the <u>same</u> <u>primary school</u>. Our mothers saw that we looked a bit <u>similar</u> and then they started dressing us the same way. We got the same <u>haircut</u> and that is how everything began.
Kim: We have got the same hobbies and we buy the same clothes. We wear the same tattoos and the same <u>tongue</u> piercings. We both play the guitar and want to <u>join</u> a girls' band one day.
Moderator: Which hobbies have you got?
Carrie: We love windsurfing and stand up <u>paddle boarding</u> in the summer and in the winter we like skiing. And we are in the same jazz dance club, of course. We do everything together. Even if we read a book, we <u>choose</u> the same.
Moderator: And do you spend your holidays together?
Kim: Yes, <u>mostly</u>. <u>Since</u> our parents are best friends, our families spend a lot of time together.
Moderator: And have you ever had an <u>argument</u>?
Carrie: Oh yes, we have. That's <u>quite</u> normal, isn't it? But <u>generally</u>, we <u>get on well with</u> each other.
Kim: Yes, we have got a good <u>relationship</u> and we help each other whenever we can.
Carrie: Yes, this is what friends are for.
Moderator: And how about a boyfriend?
Kim: We haven't got boyfriends yet. But I think we have got the same <u>taste</u> in boys. <u>Perhaps</u> we <u>might</u> find twin brothers one day.
Moderator: What plans have you got for your future?
Carrie: We want to study music and <u>share</u> a <u>flat</u>.
Moderator: And how about your mothers? Do they <u>resemble</u> each other?
Kim: No, they don't. It's just a nice <u>coincidence</u> that we <u>look alike</u>.
Moderator: Thank you for coming to our studio.
Kim and Carrie: Thank you for having us.

welcome	begrüßen	*argument*	Streit
look like	aussehen wie	*quite*	ganz
twins	Zwillinge	*generally*	im Allgemeinen
not even	nicht einmal	*get on well with*	gut auskommen mit
same	gleich	*relationship*	Beziehung
primary school	Volksschule	*taste*	Geschmack
similar	ähnlich	*perhaps*	vielleicht
haircut	Haarschnitt	*might*	vielleicht können
tongue	Zunge	*share*	teilen
join	mitmachen / beitreten	*flat*	Wohnung
paddle boarding	Paddeln	*resemble*	sich ähneln
choose	wählen	*coincidence*	Zufall
mostly	meistens	*look alike*	gleich aussehen
since	da		

1. F (They aren't sisters.)
2. F (since primary school)
3. T
4. T
5. F (not always but mostly)

6. F (They sometimes have an argument.)
7. T
8. F (They haven't got boyfriends yet.)
9. T
10. F (They don't resemble each other.)

37 Listen to the pupils talking about their favourite film directors and **match** (füge zusammen) **the sentence halves** (die Satzhälften):

Elisa: My favourite <u>film director</u> is <u>definitely</u> Alfred Hitchcock. He is called "The <u>Master</u> of <u>Suspense</u>" and he really is. <u>Moreover</u>, his <u>movies</u> are full of <u>wit</u> and they are famous for their excellent <u>storylines</u>. My favourite films are *Psycho*, filmed in black-and-white, *Vertigo* and *The Birds*. Some scenes are so <u>scary</u> that you sit in front of the <u>telly</u> <u>trembling</u>. You feel that something terrible is going to happen and there is this <u>frightening</u> music. Most of his characters have got a <u>strange</u> <u>relationship</u> with their mothers, sometimes too <u>close</u> or full of conflicts. What I find good fun is that Hitchcock himself sometimes <u>turns up</u> in a <u>scene</u>. There he is crossing a street or waiting for the bus or sitting in a café reading a newspaper. He really is a great <u>artist</u>, <u>perhaps</u> the greatest of all time. And Robert, who's your favourite director?

Robert: Well, let me think for a moment. The film director I like best is Ridley Scott. He is a master of <u>historical</u> drama but also of science fiction and <u>war</u> films. He has been very <u>successful</u> in each <u>genre</u>. All of his films have great music and excellent fight scenes and of course great <u>visual effects</u>. The films I like most are *Gladiator*, a great historical film, *Alien*, a science fiction film, *Black Hawk*, which is a war film, then *Blade Runner* and *Kingdom of Heaven*, and of course *Hannibal*. I really can't tell you which film is my favourite. Adya, which film director do you <u>prefer</u>?

Adya: My top favourite film director is Uprenda Rao. He comes from India. I like him a lot because all of his films have got a very important <u>message</u>. He does not want to <u>entertain</u> or make money with his movies. His films are realistic and each film has got a different, sometimes very <u>unusual</u> story. The film I like best is *Om*. It tells the story about gangsters in Bangalore. What I find <u>fascinating</u> is that real gangsters were in the film. The message of the film is "<u>peace</u>". I also like *Super* and *Shhh!*, which is a very scary thriller. Ah, yes, I <u>nearly</u> forgot his film about the <u>meaning</u> of love, *A*. Have you ever heard about Uprenda?

Robert: No, <u>unfortunately</u> not.

film director	Regisseur	*artist*	Künstler
definitely	auf jeden Fall	*perhaps*	vielleicht
master	Meister	*historical*	historisch
suspense	Spannung	*war*	Krieg
moreover	außerdem	*successful*	erfolgreich
movie	Film	*genre*	Gattung
wit	Witz / Geist	*visual effect*	visueller Effekt
storyline	Handlung	*prefer*	vorziehen
scary	furchterregend	*message*	Botschaft
telly	Fernseher	*entertain*	unterhalten
trembling	zitternd	*unusual*	ungewöhnlich
frightening	furchterregend	*fascinating*	faszinierend
strange	seltsam	*peace*	Frieden
relationship	Beziehung	*nearly*	fast
close	eng	*meaning*	Bedeutung
turn up	auftauchen	*unfortunately*	unglücklicherweise
scene	Szene		

1. g
2. e
3. h
4. i
5. j

6. b
7. a
8. d
9. f
10. c

38 Listen to Max talking about his favourite film and **tick the correct answers**:

Interviewer:	Max, what is your favourite film?
Max:	Well, that's hard to say because there are many films I really <u>adore</u>. But the film I like best at the moment is *Teenage Gangsters*.
Interviewer:	What is it about?
Max:	It is about a group of five boys who <u>punish</u> gangsters and help the police catch the <u>criminals</u>. Of course the boys are no gangsters, so the <u>title</u> is a bit <u>misleading</u>.
Interviewer:	Aren't there any girls in the film?
Max:	No, that's the <u>amazing</u> thing. It's just boys. There are no <u>parts</u> for girls or women in the film.
Interviewer:	And <u>of course</u> there is a happy ending.
Max:	<u>Unfortunately</u> there isn't. It's a very sad ending, which I don't like at all. But the film <u>on the whole</u> is really good. It's full of <u>wit</u> and <u>tension</u> and there are some <u>unexpected</u> <u>twists</u> in the story.

adore	sehr gerne mögen	*of course*	natürlich
punish	betrafen	*unfortunately*	unglücklicherweise
criminal	Krimineller	*on the whole*	im Großen und Ganzen
title	Titel	*wit*	Witz
misleading	irreführend	*tension*	Spannung
amazing	erstaunlich	*unexpected*	unerwartet
part	Rolle	*twist*	Wendung

1. b
2. c

3. a
4. b

39 Listen to Katie talking about her favourite film and **circle the correct options** (Möglichkeiten):

My favourite film is *The Candle*. It's a horror thriller with science fiction elements. The <u>director</u> used lots of <u>special effects</u>. For example, he filmed the most horrible scenes in black and white. The <u>screenplay</u> was <u>gripping</u> and <u>scary</u>. No second was <u>boring</u>. Sometimes the story was so real and then, in the next minute, something quite <u>unusual happened</u>. The <u>actors</u> were really <u>brilliant</u>, <u>especially</u> the girl who played the part of the <u>mysterious</u> Sally. Her name is Sophia

Lansbury and she has become a very <u>successful</u> star. I <u>wonder</u> if she was <u>frightened</u> herself when she had to play a scary scene. And she was so good-looking with her white face, in her long white dress and with the candle in her hands. Sally is <u>trapped</u> in a <u>wooden</u> box by day. If somebody opens the box, he will find a normal wooden <u>doll</u>. But when it is dark, she <u>comes to life</u>. Then she has got <u>supernatural</u> <u>powers</u> and <u>takes</u> terrible <u>revenge</u> on people who are not nice to children. You can follow the girl's <u>thoughts</u>. It's kind of like <u>entering</u> her <u>brain</u>. You can really see what Sally thinks. And the scenes explaining her thoughts are computer-<u>generated</u>. A <u>splendid</u> idea which I have never seen before in a film. The music is <u>awesome</u>, too. The <u>composer</u> had so many <u>extraordinary</u> ideas and you are always <u>surprised</u> by what comes next. Sometimes there is a nice <u>nursery rhyme</u> that slowly <u>develops</u> into a <u>hair-raising</u> song and ends up in a <u>shrill</u> sound. It's a very special film. It is for <u>viewers</u> <u>aged</u> 16 and over but I watched it together with my elder brother and he told me to <u>close</u> my eyes before a very scary scene. I cannot <u>recommend</u> watching it alone.

candle	Kerze	*supernatural*	übernatürlich
director	Regisseur	*power*	Kraft
special effect	Spezialeffekt	*take revenge*	sich rächen
screenplay	Drehbuch	*thought*	Gedanke
gripping	fesselnd	*enter*	betreten
scary	furchterregend	*brain*	Gehirn
boring	langweilig	*generated*	erzeugt
unusual	ungewöhnlich	*splendid*	großartig
happen	passieren	*awesome*	fantastisch
actor	Schauspieler	*composer*	Komponist
brilliant	hervorragend	*extraordinary*	außergewöhnlich
especially	besonders	*surprised*	überrascht
mysterious	geheimnisvoll	*nursery rhyme*	Kinderlied
successful	erfolgreich	*develop*	sich entwickeln
wonder	wissen wollen	*hair-raising*	haarsträubend
be frightened	sich fürchten	*shrill*	schrill
trapped	gefangen	*viewer*	Zuschauer
wooden	aus Holz	*aged*	im Alter von
doll	Puppe	*close*	schließen
come to life	zum Leben erwachen	*recommend*	empfehlen

1. **horror thriller**
2. **director** (director = Regisseur, headmaster = Schuldirektor)
3. **black and white**
4. **screenplay** (screenplay = Drehbuch, play = Theaterstück), **scary** (scary = furchterregend, scared = verängstigt)
5. **boring** (boring = langweilig, bored = gelangweilt)
6. **quite** (quite = ganz, quiet = ruhig)
7. **star**
8. **white** (white = weiß, weird = seltsam)
9. **wooden** (wooden = aus Holz, woollen = wollen / aus Wolle)
10. **life** (life = Leben, live = leben)
11. **people**
12. **enter** (enter = betreten, entertain = unterhalten)
13. **awesome** (awesome = großartig, awful = schrecklich)
14. **surprised** (surprised = überrascht, surprising = überraschend)
15. **sound**
16. **over 16**

40 Listen to Emma talking about her favourite video game and **circle T** (True) or **F** (False):

Shangri-La is my favourite video game. It <u>means</u> "paradise". The game has got excellent graphics and the people look so real. This game <u>beats</u> all the <u>violent</u> games! It was <u>released</u> in January 2018. The sounds are great, no <u>boring</u> "bleep, bleep". It's fantastic and I'm sure it will be a great <u>success</u>. When playing it you have to be quick and you must have perfect concentration. You have to think a lot and the story is very interesting. <u>Moreover</u>, you have to be good at calculating and counting. That's a good exercise. It's not a shooter game. Actually, you never shoot or defeat enemies and there are no gushes of blood. That's what I like most about the game. You have to collect points and useful keys. You receive them for solving puzzles. The aim of this game is to destroy the kingdom of darkness through smart decisions and create a new paradise. You save people, mostly children and animals and lead them to places of safety where no evil can enter. Each game has a time limit of 30 minutes.

Thus you are forced to stop and there is no danger of getting hooked on the game, so you don't play endlessly. You can play it alone or in multi-player. It's a game your parents will like, too. I can warmly recommend it.

What I find most amazing is that Bernie Bail, the creator of the game, is a Mennonite and gives away half of the income to help poor people.

mean	bedeuten	darkness	Dunkelheit
beat	schlagen / besser sein	smart	klug
violent	gewalttätig	decision	Entscheidung
released	veröffentlicht	create	schaffen
boring	langweilig	save	retten
success	Erfolg	mostly	hauptsächlich
moreover	darüber hinaus	lead	führen
calculate	rechnen	safety	Sicherheit
count	zählen	evil	Böses
shooter	Schieß-	enter	eindringen
actually	tatsächlich	thus	auf diese Weise
defeat	besiegen	forced	gezwungen
enemy	Feind	hooked on	süchtig nach
gush	Schwall	multi-player	für mehrere Spieler
useful	nützlich	warmly	wärmstens
key	Schlüssel	recommend	empfehlen
receive	erhalten	amazing	erstaunlich
solve	lösen	creator	Schöpfer
puzzle	Rätsel	Mennonite	Mennonit
aim	Ziel	income	Einkommen
destroy	zerstören	poor	arm
kingdom	Königreich		

1. F (It means "paradise".)
2. T
3. F (The game beats all violent games.)
4. T
5. T
6. T
7. T
8. F (good at calculating and counting)
9. F (It isn't a shooter game.)
10. F (that there are no gushes of blood)
11. F (You don't buy them. You get them for solving puzzles.)
12. T
13. T
14. F (There is a time limit of 30 minutes.)
15. T
16. F (half of his income)

41 Listen to the radio programme *Teens Speak Out* **and answer the questions:**

Moderator: Good afternoon to all our listeners. Today's question is "What is best about being a teenager?"
And here is our first caller. It's Holly, isn't it?
Holly: Exactly. For me the best about being 13 is that I get more pocket money.
Moderator: And what do you do with your pocket money? What do you spend it on?
Holly: I save part of my money for riding lessons and what remains I spend on books, clothes, CDs, video games and stuff.
Moderator: Are you allowed to go to parties?
Holly: Yes, I am, but only in the afternoons, like birthday parties or garden parties. I'm not allowed to come home later than 8 p.m. But for me that's OK.
Moderator: Are you allowed to go into chat rooms?
Holly: Yes, I am. I have some Facebook friends and we share photos and messages. But I'm not allowed to meet my contacts before asking my parents because that might

be <u>dangerous</u>. My parents want to know who I meet and where I am. My friend Elisa once wanted to meet a cool <u>guy</u> she got to know over the Internet but that cool guy <u>turned out</u> to be a 42-year-old man. That was really dangerous for her.

Moderator: What else is nice about being a teenager?

Holly: What I really like is that I'm allowed to buy my own clothes. My mum and I haven't got the <u>same</u> <u>taste</u> in clothes and now I can buy what I want. <u>Moreover</u>, I may even <u>dye</u> my hair blue or green if I want to. But I'm not allowed to <u>stuff</u> myself with fast food all the time. And I'm not allowed to have a <u>stud</u> or piercings without asking my parents first. But I'm sure they would say "no" to a <u>tattoo</u> or things like that.

Moderator: I can <u>imagine</u> that.

Holly: Oh yes, I'm allowed to <u>invite</u> friends over or sleep at a friend's place but only when my parents or my friends' parents are in. But that's alright for me.

Moderator: Thanks for calling, Holly. Thank you for listening and <u>join</u> us again next week.

listener	Zuhörer	guy	Junge
caller	Anrufer	turn out	sich herausstellen
exactly	genau	same	gleich
pocket money	Taschengeld	taste	Geschmack
spend on	ausgeben für	moreover	außerdem
save	sparen	dye	färben
part	Teil	stuff	sich vollstopfen
remain	bleiben	stud	Stecker in der Nase
stuff	Dinge / Zeug	tattoo	Tätowierung
be allowed to	dürfen	imagine	sich vorstellen
share	teilen	invite	einladen
might	könnte vielleicht	join	dabei sein
dangerous	gefährlich		

1. The best thing for her is that she gets more pocket money.
2. She spends her money on books, clothes, CDs, video games and stuff / and other things.
3. She saves part of her money for riding lessons.
4. Not later than 8 p.m.
5. She shares photos and messages with them.
6. Because it might be dangerous.
7. He was a 42-year-old man.
8. She is allowed to buy her own clothes. / She is allowed to buy books, clothes, CDs, video games and stuff / and other things.
9. Because her mum and she haven't got the same taste in clothes.
10. She is not allowed to stuff herself with fast food.
11. She is not allowed to have a stud, piercings or a tattoo.
12. She is allowed to invite friends over or sleep at a friend's place.

42 Listen to Riley and **tick** (hake ab) **what he is allowed to do:**

For me, being 13 <u>means</u> staying up later on weekends, going to the cinema with friends, meeting up at a fast food place and so on. I have to be back home <u>by</u> 9 p.m. But I still <u>mustn't</u> watch late-night films. With my older brother I'm <u>allowed to</u> go and see a football match in the evening. Then I can stay out later. I love those evenings with my brother. We have popcorn and Coke <u>during</u> the match and after we always go to a fast food place. <u>Moreover</u>, I can invite friends to our house but my room must be clean and <u>tidy</u>. That's a must. I'm allowed to cook with my friends but the kitchen must be clean after cooking. I<u>'m into</u> cooking, you know, and I'm really good at it. I'm not allowed to drink any alcohol, <u>not even</u> when my parents are around. What I find cool is that I'm allowed to use my parents' camera and I have taken lots of really good pictures <u>so far</u>. I want to make a <u>calendar</u> with the photos for my grandparents for Christmas. But there are still many things I'm not allowed to do, like for example, <u>stuff</u> myself with sweets and eat hamburgers and chips more often than <u>once a week</u>, play video games for more than two hours a day, wear an earring and turn the music up loud when my parents are home. And <u>finally</u>, there is an absolute "no" to <u>hanging out with</u> kids my parents don't know. But that's OK for me. <u>On the whole</u>, my parents are cool.

mean	bedeuten	*not even*	nicht einmal
by	bis spätestens	*so far*	bis jetzt
mustn't	nicht dürfen	*calendar*	Kalender
be allowed to	dürfen	*stuff*	sich vollstopfen
during	während	*once a week*	einmal pro Woche
moreover	außerdem	*finally*	schließlich
tidy	ordentlich	*hang out with*	herumhängen mit
be into	etwas sehr gerne tun	*on the whole*	im Großen und Ganzen

1, 2, 5, 6, 7, 9, 12

43 Listen to Ruby talking about her family and **match** (füge zusammen) **the sentence halves** (die Satzhälften):

For me, being 13 now hasn't changed anything. The rules in our family are still the <u>same</u>. My parents are very <u>strict</u>. My sister and I are not <u>allowed to</u> <u>enter</u> the living room with shoes on. Our shoes must be <u>left</u> in the hall. We are not allowed to make a <u>mess</u> in the kitchen. When my mum comes home from work, the kitchen must be clean. We're not allowed to eat in the living room or up in our rooms. My mum is <u>dead against</u> <u>TV dinners</u>. We are only allowed to eat in the kitchen or in the small <u>dining room</u>, <u>though</u> in the summertime, we often have <u>barbecues</u> in the garden. We must clean out the <u>cage</u> of our <u>budgie</u> <u>regularly</u> and we have to help in the garden. That means watering the flowers and <u>weeding</u> and <u>mowing</u> the grass. My parents come home as late as six or seven p.m. so we all have to help with the housework. We are not allowed to play ball games in the part of the garden where the roses <u>grow</u>, and our parents are very strict about our school things. Our books and notebooks must be clean and without <u>dog-ears</u>, <u>stains</u> or <u>scribbling</u>. My dad is a teacher and he hates when we are <u>careless</u> about our school things.

same	gleich	*cage*	Käfig
strict	streng	*budgie*	Wellensittich
be allowed to	dürfen	*regularly*	regelmäßig
enter	betreten	*weed*	Unkraut jäten
left	gelassen	*mow*	mähen
mess	Unordnung	*grow*	wachsen
dead against	total dagegen	*dog-ear*	Eselsohr
TV dinner	beim Fernsehen essen	*stain*	Fleck
dining room	Esszimmer	*scribbling*	Kritzelei
though	jedoch	*careless*	schlampig
barbecue	Grillfest		

1. h   9. k
2. f   10. e
3. n   11. c
4. a   12. i
5. m   13. j
6. l   14. d
7. b   15. g
8. p   16. o

44 Listen to the radio programme *Meet the World* and **circle** (kreise ein) **T** (True) or **F** (False):

Moderator:	Good evening to all our <u>listeners</u>. Welcome to our radio programme *Meet the World*. And here is our first <u>caller</u>. It's Samuel from Pennsylvania, isn't it?
Samuel:	Yes, it is.
Moderator:	Hi Samuel! Tell us about your life!
Samuel:	I'm a <u>member</u> of an <u>Amish group</u>. We <u>mostly</u> live and work like our <u>great-grandfathers</u> did. But in our group we have got <u>electricity</u>, mobile phones and a new tractor.
Moderator:	That's interesting! Does that mean you don't have any TV, video games, or Internet?

Samuel:	We haven't got a TV at home and I haven't got any video games, but at school we have got a computer and the Internet. So we know what is going on <u>outside</u> our group.
Moderator:	Isn't your life very <u>boring</u>?
Samuel:	No, it isn't. There is always a lot of work to do. I go to school and in the afternoon I help with the work on the farm. We still don't have cars but we have got lots of horses. Most important in our group is our family and the <u>community</u>. We help <u>each other</u> and we are very <u>peaceful</u> <u>people</u>. So, I will never <u>join the army</u>.
Moderator:	Are you interested in the <u>latest fashions</u>?
Samuel:	No, I am not. I would say we dress in a very <u>old-fashioned</u> way and the girls never cut or <u>dye</u> their hair or wear rings, <u>bracelets</u> or <u>necklaces</u>. Most men in our community wear long <u>beards</u>.
Moderator:	Have you got any brothers or sisters?
Samuel:	Yes, I have four brothers and one sister. I am the <u>eldest</u>.
Moderator:	Which <u>languages</u> do you speak?
Samuel:	My <u>mother tongue</u> is Pennsylvania German but I have also been learning English at school.
Moderator:	What are your plans for your <u>future</u>, Samuel? Will you always stay in your <u>village</u>?
Samuel:	When I'm older I will spend one year in New York away from my group. This year is called "rumspringa" which means "run around". In that year I will get to know the modern way of life. After that year I must <u>decide</u> if I want to join my Amish group again or stay in the modern world. But I'm sure I'm not going to <u>leave</u> my <u>church</u>. I'm going to come back and I want to have a restaurant for the tourists that come and visit our village.
Moderator:	That was very interesting. Thank you for calling, Samuel.
Samuel:	You're welcome.

listener	Zuhörer	*latest fashion*	neueste Mode
caller	Anrufer	*old-fashioned*	altmodisch
member	Mitglied	*dye*	färben
Amish group	amische Gruppe (Religionsgemeinschaft)	*bracelet*	Armband
		necklace	Halskette
mostly	hauptsächlich	*beard*	Bart
great-grandfather	Urgroßvater	*eldest*	älteste / -r / -s
electricity	Elektrizität	*language*	Sprache
outside	außerhalb	*mother tongue*	Muttersprache
boring	langweilig	*future*	Zukunft
community	Gemeinschaft	*village*	Dorf
each other	einander	*decide*	entscheiden
peaceful	friedlich	*leave*	verlassen
people	Leute	*church*	Kirche
join the army	der Armee beitreten		

1. T
2. F (They have got a TV at school and he hasn't got any video games.)
3. T
4. F (His life isn't boring because he has got lots of work to do.)
5. T
6. F (no cars)
7. T
8. F (He won't join the army because his group is very peaceful.)

9. F (He isn't.)
10. T
11. F (They don't.)
12. T
13. T
14. T
15. F (New York)
16. F (He is going to come back to his group.)
17. T

45 Listen to the phone-in show *Meet the World* and **circle** (kreise ein) **T** (True) or **F** (False):

Moderator:	And our <u>guest</u> today is a <u>caller</u> from Sydney, Australia. Welcome to our show *Meet the World*.
Benan:	Hi. My name is Benan, which <u>means</u> Toby in English. I live in Sydney with my parents.

We are <u>Aboriginal people</u>. My dad is a <u>lawyer</u> and my mum is a teacher. Some of my <u>relatives</u> live in the Northern Territory of Australia. What I'd like to tell you about my people is that most of them are really <u>poor</u> and their <u>living conditions</u> are very bad. Some live on <u>reservations</u> and have no work. They smoke and drink too much. They <u>suffer from</u> <u>heart diseases</u> and <u>develop</u> <u>lung</u> and <u>liver</u> <u>cancer</u>. Aboriginal people die ten years earlier <u>on average</u> than non-Aboriginal people. Many of them <u>commit suicide</u>. What they really need is clean water, <u>healthy</u> food, <u>vaccination</u>, better <u>healthcare</u> and better <u>education</u>.

Moderator:	That's a sad story.
Benan:	Yes, it is. That's why I want to study medicine and go back to the Northern Territory to help my people.
Moderator:	What <u>languages</u> do they speak?
Benan:	There are around 150 different Aboriginal languages that are still <u>in use</u> but most of us speak English today.
Moderator:	Have you got any hobbies? Do you play football, for example?
Benan:	No, I don't. My favourite hobby is taking photographs. I love taking pictures of my people in their traditional way of living. And I love <u>painting</u> and <u>drawing</u>. I draw the faces and bodies painted in white of Aboriginal people but I also paint <u>drunk</u> men with <u>bottles</u> in their hands. <u>Moreover</u>, I love drawing old motifs and <u>patterns</u> of <u>rock paintings</u>. And <u>of course</u> I am <u>fascinated</u> by our <u>holy</u> mountain Ayers Rock.
Moderator:	I can <u>imagine</u> that this beautiful mountain is a wonderful motif for painters and photographers.
Benan:	Yes, it is. But one of my best photos is an Aboriginal boy holding a boomerang in one hand and a mobile phone in the other. It was shown at an <u>exhibition</u>.
Moderator:	That's wonderful! <u>Congratulations</u>! <u>Unfortunately</u>, time is up again. Thank you very much for calling, Benan and for all that interesting information you gave to our <u>listeners</u>.
Benan:	<u>You're welcome</u>.

guest	Gast	*education*	Ausbildung
caller	Anrufer	*language*	Sprache
mean	bedeuten	*in use*	in Verwendung
Aboriginal people	Aborigines / Ureinwohner Australiens	*painting*	Malen
lawyer	Jurist	*drawing*	Zeichnen
relative	Verwandte / -r	*drunk*	betrunken
poor	arm	*bottle*	Flasche
living condition	Lebensbedingung	*moreover*	außerdem
reservation	Reservat	*pattern*	Muster
suffer from	leiden an	*rock painting*	Felsmalerei
heart disease	Herzkrankheit	*of course*	natürlich
develop	entwickeln	*fascinated*	fasziniert
lung	Lunge	*holy*	heilig
liver	Leber	*imagine*	sich vorstellen
cancer	Krebs	*exhibition*	Ausstellung
on average	im Durchschnitt	*Congratulations!*	Glückwunsch! / Gratuliere!
commit suicide	Selbstmord begehen	*unfortunately*	unglücklicherweise
healthy	gesund	*listener*	Zuhörer
vaccination	Impfung	*You're welcome.*	Gern geschehen.
healthcare	medizinische Versorgung		

1. T
2. T
3. F (Northern Territory)
4. T
5. T
6. F (They die earlier.)
7. T
8. T
9. T
10. F (taking photos, painting, drawing)
11. T
12. F (He also draws drunk men.)
13. T
14. T
15. T
16. F (One of his photos was shown at an exhibition.)

46 Listen to Chloe talking about life in Tehran and **tick the correct answers**:

Interviewer:	Chloe, why did you <u>move</u> to <u>Tehran</u>?
Chloe:	My father is an <u>engineer</u> and his <u>firm</u> sent him to Tehran for three years. So our whole family moved. My brother and I go to an international school and it is great to meet so many different pupils from different countries. The only poor one is my mum.
Interviewer:	Why is your mum poor?
Chloe:	Because she had to give up her job as an architect at home. But she will take up her job <u>as soon as</u> we <u>return</u>.
Interviewer:	How is your life different from back home?
Chloe:	It is totally different. At home I can go everywhere <u>whenever</u> I want to. That is not possible in Tehran for a girl. For example I'm not allowed to go shopping all alone. And when I want to visit a friend from school, my mother or my brother has to <u>accompany</u> me there. <u>Imagine</u>! My brother has more <u>rights</u> than me! He can go out alone! He <u>enjoys</u> more <u>freedom</u> than me and that is unfair! And there is the <u>dress code</u>. I always have to wear a long coat with long <u>sleeves</u> and a <u>scarf</u> even if it is very hot.
Interviewer:	What do you like best about your life in Tehran?
Chloe:	Hm. That's a difficult question. There are so many things I like. I love going out to restaurants with my family. The food is great. Then I love visiting the <u>mosques</u> together with my mum. I love the atmosphere there and my mum <u>is into</u> the <u>tiles</u> with their beautiful <u>patterns</u>. She talks about the <u>architecture</u> of the mosques and tells me lots of interesting things. And I love the markets. Imagine those <u>various</u> kinds of fruit and vegetables. But what I like most is <u>definitely</u> that it is easy to make new friends because everybody is interested in my culture and my way of life back home. Even if I wear a scarf, everybody knows from the very first moment that I'm not <u>Iranian</u>. I have got blue eyes and light brown <u>eyebrows</u>. And of course my English accent is different. Any more questions?
Interviewer:	Yes. Chloe, would you like to stay in Tehran <u>forever</u>?
Chloe:	I don't think so. I <u>miss</u> my old school friends and our <u>neighbours</u>. And I miss, please don't laugh, some of my teachers. Now I see that they were really cool. But I <u>mostly</u> miss my grandparents.
Interviewer:	Last question: What are your plans for the future?
Chloe:	Back home I'd like to study architecture and <u>join</u> my mother's <u>company</u>. But my brother thinks I'll be a <u>female rights</u> activist.
Interviewer:	Thank you so much for talking to me.
Chloe:	It was a <u>pleasure</u>.

move	übersiedeln	*be into*	sehr gerne mögen
Tehran	Teheran	*tile*	Fliese
engineer	Ingenieur	*pattern*	Muster
firm	Firma	*architecture*	Architektur
as soon as	sobald als	*various*	verschiedenartig
return	zurückkehren	*definitely*	zweifellos
whenever	immer wenn	*Iranian*	Iraner / -in
accompany	begleiten	*eyebrow*	Augenbraue
imagine	sich vorstellen	*forever*	für immer
right	Recht	*miss*	vermissen
enjoy	genießen	*neighbour*	Nachbar
freedom	Freiheit	*mostly*	hauptsächlich
dress code	Dresscode	*join*	eintreten in
sleeve	Ärmel	*company*	Firma
scarf	Schal / Kopftuch	*female rights*	Frauenrechte
mosque	Moschee	*pleasure*	Vergnügen

1.	b	4.	d
2.	b	5.	c
3.	c	6.	a

70

47 Listen to Theo talking about his new neighbour and **circle** (kreise ein) **T** (True) or **F** (False):

Theo: We have got a new <u>neighbour</u>.
Ellie: Oh. Is he nice? Has he got children?
Theo: No, he isn't nice and he hasn't got children. He is very old and <u>grumpy</u> and doesn't like children. Seven days after moving in, he <u>handed</u> us a list of what we were not <u>allowed</u> to do.
Ellie: You'<u>re kidding</u>! What was there on the list?
Theo: The list said that we weren't allowed to play football in our garden because he didn't like the <u>noise</u>.
Ellie: You cannot be <u>serious</u>!
Theo: From now on we aren't allowed to sing and shout and jump into our <u>pond</u>. My brother isn't allowed to play the piano after 6 pm. My sister isn't allowed to climb the old <u>oak tree</u> because then she <u>might</u> <u>be able to</u> look into his garden. Our cat isn't allowed to climb over the <u>fence</u> and jump into his garden.
Ellie: But your cat doesn't understand that!
Theo: Yes, that's the problem.
Ellie: What else was there on the list?
Theo: No mowing the grass before 3 pm. Our dog isn't allowed to play or <u>bark</u> in the garden. Dad isn't allowed to have a <u>barbecue</u> because of the <u>smoke</u> and the <u>smell</u>. But the best is that my mum isn't allowed to invite her friends for an afternoon tea because he can't stand their <u>chattering</u>. That was the only point where my dad <u>applauded</u>.
Ellie: Yes, that last point is great fun. But what are you going to do against that grumpy old man?
Theo: My sister and I want to send him a <u>leaflet</u> on children's <u>rights</u>. Then we want to go on a <u>protest march</u> in front of his house together with all of our friends. Or we could play <u>tricks</u> on him. My sister wants to put a <u>spell</u> on him. But my mum and my dad want to find a <u>peaceful</u> solution. They are planning on inviting him for a barbecue and I should <u>offer</u> to help him in the garden if he needs anybody. Mum is going to offer to go shopping for him. And she thinks it might be a good idea that he <u>gets to know</u> our cat and our dog. <u>Perhaps</u> he'll start to like them and perhaps even <u>pet</u> them. Our pets can be very nice and <u>charming</u>. Dad thinks it might be great if I played some music on my piano for him. And mum wants to invite him for a cup of tea and a piece of cake when her <u>chatterboxes</u> are around.
Ellie: That sounds great. Perhaps he is only a poor, old and <u>lonely</u> man. Perhaps he needs a family. I wish you good luck with your grandfather project.
Theo: Thanks a lot.

neighbour	Nachbar	*chattering*	Gequassel
grumpy	missmutig	*applaud*	applaudieren
hand	überreichen	*leaflet*	Broschüre / Flugblatt
be allowed	dürfen	*right*	Recht
be kidding	Witze machen	*protest march*	Demonstration
noise	Lärm	*trick*	Streich
serious	ernst	*spell*	Fluch
pond	Teich	*peaceful*	friedlich
oak tree	Eiche	*solution*	Lösung
might	könnte vielleicht	*offer*	anbieten
be able to	können	*get to know*	kennenlernen
fence	Zaun	*perhaps*	vielleicht
bark	bellen	*pet*	streicheln
barbecue	Grillfest	*charming*	charmant
smoke	Rauch	*chatterbox*	Plaudertasche
smell	Geruch	*lonely*	einsam

1.   F (He is grumpy and doesn't like children.)   5.   F (He isn't allowed to make a barbecue.)
2.   T   6.   T
3.   F (play football)   7.   T
4.   T

48 Listen to the children talking about their school cafeteria and **match** (füge zusammen) **the sentence halves** (die Satzhälften):

Stuart: <u>Yuck</u>. I hate our <u>school cafeteria</u>. Look! There's only <u>trash</u>: doughnuts, hamburgers, pizzas, chips, puddings, <u>chocolate bars</u>, cakes and <u>soft drinks</u>. Nothing really <u>healthy</u>.

Sofia: You're right. I always take my own lunch with me because I can't buy anything here at school.

Stuart: They should <u>offer</u> healthy things like vegetables and fruits. There are so many <u>vegetarians</u> here at school and they can't buy anything in our cafeteria.

Sofia: We should ask the <u>manager</u> of the cafeteria for a new and healthier <u>menu</u>. And let's inform our <u>headmaster</u>.

Stuart: You're right. I'm sure he is interested and wants to help us. We can organize a group for better school lunches. Let's put up a new menu with healthy food. There should be <u>less</u> meat and more vegetables and fruits. We can also write posters with our <u>suggestions</u>. <u>Moreover</u>, we can organize an online <u>poll</u> where all our <u>mates</u> can <u>choose</u> from <u>various meals</u>.

Sofia: Good idea! And we can <u>hand out</u> <u>leaflets</u> and make a Power Point presentation about what soft drinks and <u>especially</u> Coke does to our bodies. <u>Imagine</u>, there are 40 <u>lumps of sugar</u> in one litre of Coke! That can't be healthy!

Stuart: You're right. Let's ask all our friends to help us.

yuck	pfui	*suggestion*	Vorschlag
school cafeteria	Schulbuffet	*moreover*	außerdem
trash	wertloses Zeug	*poll*	Abstimmung
chocolate bar	Schokoriegel	*mate*	Schulkamerad
soft drink	Limonade	*choose*	wählen
healthy	gesund	*various*	verschieden
offer	anbieten	*meal*	Speise
vegetarian	Vegetarier	*hand out*	austeilen
manager	Leiter	*leaflet*	Flugblatt
menu	Speiseplan	*especially*	besonders
headmaster	Schuldirektor	*imagine*	sich vorstellen
less	weniger	*lump of sugar*	Würfelzucker

1. e
2. h
3. j
4. a
5. i

6. b
7. c
8. d
9. f
10. g

49 Listen to the interview about Freddie's protest group and **circle** (kreise ein) **T** (True) or **F** (False):

Scarlett: May I ask you <u>a few</u> questions about your protest group for our <u>school magazine</u>?

Freddie: <u>Of course</u>, <u>go ahead</u>.

Scarlett: What are you and your group fighting against?

Freddie: We're fighting against the bar next to the kindergarten.

Scarlett: What's so bad about the bar?

Freddie: <u>Imagine</u> all that <u>dirt</u> that the <u>guests</u> of the bar <u>leave behind</u>. Every morning the <u>pavement</u> and the street are full of <u>litter</u>, broken bottles and glass and there's lots of paper around. And guests that are <u>drunk</u> sing or shout loudly. For me, that is <u>another</u> form of <u>pollution</u>. It's <u>noise</u> pollution. When I take my little brother to kindergarten we have to walk over broken glass and through <u>waste paper</u> and cigarette <u>butts</u>.

Scarlett: That's <u>gross</u>! That is <u>worth</u> fighting against!

Freddie: Yes, it is.

Scarlett: When did you <u>found</u> the group?

Freddie: Three weeks ago and we have been very active <u>since</u>.

Scarlett: What <u>measures</u> have you taken <u>so far</u>?

Freddie: First we tried to talk to the <u>owner</u> of the bar but he only said "You are too young for the bar. Come again in five years." Then he laughed at us and threw us out of the bar. Then we wrote a letter to the <u>mayor</u>. We also <u>handed out</u> <u>leaflets</u> to inform people about the situation. Last week we went from house to house and asked people to <u>sign</u> our <u>petition</u>.

Scarlett: How many <u>signatures</u> have you got now?

Freddie: More than 2000, I <u>guess</u>. Then we organised a <u>protest march</u> in front of the bar. There were 200 pupils from our school. It was a big <u>success</u>. And for next Monday we've organised a <u>meeting</u> with the mayor, the owner of the bar, and our group and there we are going to <u>hand over</u> our petition and a list of <u>proposals</u> on how to <u>solve</u> the problem.

Scarlett: What <u>solutions</u> to the problem are you going to <u>suggest</u>?

Freddie: The bar has to close at 10 p.m. More police should be around in this area. The owner of the bar has to clean the pavement and the street after <u>closing time</u>. There should be containers for waste paper and a <u>bottle bank</u> behind the bar. And if the owner does not <u>obey</u>, he should be <u>fined</u>.

Scarlett: Sounds great! Good luck to you and your protest group.

Freddie: Thank you.

Scarlett: How many members are there in your group?

Freddie: There are nine of us.

Scarlett: With me you are ten. I can put articles into our school magazine and the <u>local newspaper</u> to <u>support</u> you, if you want.

Freddie: That would be great! Thanks a lot!

a few	einige	*owner*	Besitzer
school magazine	Schülerzeitung	*mayor*	Bürgermeister
of course	natürlich	*hand out*	austeilen
go ahead	nur los	*leaflet*	Flugblatt
imagine	sich vorstellen	*sign*	unterzeichnen
dirt	Schmutz	*petition*	Bittschrift / Ansuchen
guest	Gast	*signature*	Unterschrift
leave behind	hinterlassen	*guess*	raten
pavement	Gehsteig	*protest march*	Demonstration
litter	Abfall	*success*	Erfolg
drunk	betrunken	*meeting*	Treffen
another	andere / -r / -s	*hand over*	überreichen
pollution	Verschmutzung	*proposal*	Vorschlag
noise	Lärm	*solve*	lösen
waste paper	Papierabfall	*solution*	Lösung
butt	Stummel	*suggest*	vorschlagen
gross	krass / ekelig	*closing time*	Sperrstunde
worth	wert	*bottle bank*	Altglascontainer
found	gründen	*obey*	gehorchen
since	seither	*fined*	mit Geldstrafe belegt
measure	Maßnahme	*local newspaper*	Lokalzeitung
so far	bis jetzt	*support*	unterstützen

1. T
2. F (They are fighting against a bar.)
3. T
4. T
5. T

6. F (three weeks ago)
7. T
8. F (He threw them out of the bar.)
9. F (200)
10. F (10 p.m.)

50 Listen to teenagers fighting against cutting down a tree and **circle** (kreise ein) **T** (True) or **F** (False):

Lola: Have you heard <u>the latest</u>? They are planning on cutting down the old <u>oak tree</u> in our town centre to build a new <u>roundabout</u>!

Kevin: That can't be true! They can't do that! What do we need a new roundabout for?

Lola: The oak tree is more than a hundred years old. People always meet at the four <u>benches</u> around the tree.

Kevin: We must do something about it. Let's organise a protest group. I'm sure that lots of people are going to help us fight against that project.

Lola: Alright. Let's organise a <u>meeting</u> with our <u>mayor</u> but first of all we must <u>prepare</u> well. We have to write a list with good <u>arguments</u> against cutting down the tree.

Kevin: Good idea. Let's begin <u>right away</u>. Write this down: The tree <u>is needed</u> for <u>fresh air</u>, for the birds, for the <u>shade</u> in the village centre. <u>Moreover</u>, it's a meeting place for old and young people.

Lola: Not so fast! What was the last argument?

Kevin: The meeting place. Then, we can <u>design</u> posters and <u>leaflets</u>.

Lola: Yes, we must hang up posters and <u>hand out</u> leaflets to inform everyone. Our <u>Art teacher</u> is going to help us, I'm sure.

Kevin: And then, if the <u>city council</u> still plans to cut down the tree, we can go on a protest march and have a <u>sit-in</u> under the tree. And Robert must go on a hunger strike.

Lola: Why Robert?

Kevin: Because he is the fattest of us.

Lola: <u>You are nuts</u>! I'm against your idea. We'd better <u>set up</u> a <u>petition</u>. Then we must go from house to house and ask people to <u>sign</u> it.

Kevin: Yes, let's do that. We also have to inform the <u>local newspaper</u> about our project. But first of all, we should ask our friends to help us.

Lola: <u>Here we go</u>!

the latest	das Neueste	*design*	entwerfen
oak tree	Eiche	*leaflet*	Flugblatt
roundabout	Kreisverkehr	*hand out*	austeilen
bench	Bank	*Art teacher*	Kunsterzieher
meeting	Treffen	*city council*	Stadtrat
mayor	Bürgermeister	*sit-in*	Sitzstreik
prepare	vorbereiten	*be nuts*	verrückt sein
argument	Argument	*set up*	aufsetzen
right away	sofort	*petition*	Bittschrift / Ansuchen
be needed	gebraucht werden	*sign*	unterzeichnen
fresh air	frische Luft	*local newspaper*	Lokalzeitung
shade	Schatten	*Here we go!*	Los geht's!
moreover	außerdem		

1. F (to build a new roundabout)
2. F (one hundred years)
3. F (four benches)
4. T
5. T
6. T
7. T
8. F (hang up posters)
9. T
10. F (the local newspaper)

51 Listen to Harvey talking about his *Protect the Planet* group and **complete** (vervollständige) **the sentences:**

Reporter: Harvey, you formed a group called *PTP*. What does that <u>mean</u>?

Harvey: It means "*Protect the Planet*".

Reporter: Are you a protest group?

Harvey: No, we aren't. We are a group of sixteen pupils from our <u>Grammar school</u>, 10 girls and six boys and our plan is to inform pupils and <u>grown-ups</u> how to <u>care</u> better for our planet, how to be <u>responsible</u>.

Reporter: That's great! How do you inform people?

Harvey: We write and <u>print</u> <u>leaflets</u> and <u>hand</u> them <u>out</u>. We <u>create</u> posters, write emails and <u>invite</u> people to <u>meetings</u> with Power Point presentations. We tell people not to <u>drop litter</u> in the streets or on the beach and to take the <u>empty</u> bottles to <u>bottle banks</u>. Then the bottles can be <u>recycled</u>. We tell them to put their old newspapers into <u>waste paper</u> <u>containers</u>. We show them what to do with empty <u>cans</u> and plastic bottles and what they are <u>used</u> for when they are recycled. We <u>advise</u> them to <u>save energy</u> and water. Our mothers even made <u>shopping bags</u> out of <u>cloth</u> and we gave them to people on the streets. They should use them <u>instead of</u> plastic bags.

Reporter: That's really great!

Harvey: Yes, we are really <u>enthusiastic</u> about our project. <u>Moreover</u> all <u>members</u> of our group always ride their bikes in the town. On all our bikes there is a slogan, "<u>Stay</u> fit and <u>healthy</u>". So, our parents never drive us <u>short distances</u>. And <u>last but not least</u> we <u>advise</u> people to buy <u>locally produced</u> food and to <u>avoid</u> fast food.

Reporter: That's really a wonderful and interesting project!

Harvey: Yes, it is. And we sometimes invite special <u>guests</u> who give talks on important <u>topics</u>. For example, <u>climate warming</u>, the <u>greenhouse effect</u>, <u>alternative energy</u> and so on. That's <u>extremely</u> interesting.

Reporter: I can <u>imagine</u> that. And who pays for all that?

Harvey: We get lots of <u>donations</u> from private people, from <u>firms</u> and so on. And most speakers talk for <u>free</u>.

Reporter: Good luck to you and your group and thank you for talking to me.

Harvey: <u>You're welcome</u>.

mean	bedeuten	*cloth*	Stoff
protect	beschützen	*instead of*	anstelle von
Grammar school	Gymnasium	*enthusiastic*	begeistert
grown-up	Erwachsener	*moreover*	außerdem
care	pflegen / sich sorgen	*member*	Mitglied
responsible	verantwortungsvoll	*stay*	bleiben
print	drucken	*healthy*	gesund
leaflet	Flugblatt	*short distance*	kurze Strecke
hand out	austeilen	*last but not least*	nicht zuletzt
create	gestalten	*advise*	raten
invite	einladen	*locally produced*	aus der Region
meeting	Treffen	*avoid*	vermeiden
drop litter	Abfall wegwerfen	*guest*	Gast
empty	leer	*topic*	Thema
bottle bank	Altglascontainer	*climate warming*	Klimaerwärmung
recycled	wiederverwertet	*greenhouse effect*	Treibhauseffekt
waste paper	Altpapier	*alternative energy*	Alternativenergie
container	Container	*extremely*	überaus
can	Dose	*imagine*	sich vorstellen
used	verwendet	*donation*	Spende
advise	raten	*firm*	Firma
save	sparen	*free*	gratis
energy	Energie	*You're welcome.*	Gern geschehen.
shopping bag	Einkaufstasche		

1. They print **leaflets** and **hand** them **out**.
2. They create **posters** and write **emails**.
3. They tell people not to **drop litter** in the streets.
4. Empty bottles should be taken to **bottle banks**.
5. They tell people to put their old newspapers into **waste** paper **containers**.
6. Bottles, old newspapers and plastic can be **recycled**.
7. People should use shopping bags made of cloth instead of **plastic**.
8. On their bikes there is a slogan, "Stay fit and **healthy**."
9. Their parents never drive them short **distances**.
10. They advise people to buy **locally produced** food.
11. They organise talks on climate **warming**, the greenhouse **effect** and alternative **energy**.
12. They get lots of **donations** from private people and from firms.

52 Listen to Ruby talking about her personal heroine and **tick the correct answers**:

Hi, I'm Ruby. For me, my personal <u>heroine</u> is my mother. She is a <u>single parent</u> because our father left us when we were still very young. He found a new wife and has two children with her, but he isn't <u>interested</u> in his old family any more. He has to pay <u>child support</u> and that's all he does. No birthday cards, no presents, no Christmas wishes, no answers to our letters. That's <u>awfully</u> <u>sad</u>, but what I find so great about my mum is that she never says bad things about our father or <u>accuses</u> him of having left us. She never <u>complains</u>. She has been working hard to give us a nice and <u>comfortable</u> home. We were <u>allowed</u> to learn to play the piano, the guitar and the <u>recorder</u>. She always took us to our music lessons when we were younger. Now we can go by bike. We always go on a camping holiday with her. One day I'd like to go on a safari holiday. That's my dream to see all the wild animals. We are also allowed to invite friends and have parties. She has really <u>managed</u> to give us a normal family life even if we don't have a lot of money. She is <u>humorous</u> and she is never <u>bad-tempered</u> or angry <u>even if</u> she sometimes has hard times in her job or with us. It's hard to <u>handle</u> three teenagers without a father. But she always has time for us and our problems. We sometimes <u>notice</u> <u>dark circles</u> around her eyes. Then we <u>hug</u> her and she smiles again. She is really my <u>idol</u>.

heroine	Heldin	*recorder*	Flöte
single parent	Alleinerzieherin	*manage*	es schaffen
interested	interessiert	*humorous*	humorvoll
child support	Unterhalt für ein Kind	*bad-tempered*	schlecht gelaunt
awfully	schrecklich	*even if*	sogar wenn
sad	traurig	*handle*	sich kümmern um
accuse	Vorwurf machen	*notice*	bemerken
complain	sich beklagen	*dark circles*	dunkle Ringe
comfortable	gemütlich	*hug*	umarmen
be allowed	dürfen	*idol*	Idol / Vorbild

1. c
2. a
3. b
4. c

5. a
6. b
7. c
8. a

53 Listen to the radio programme *Heroes and Heroines* and **circle** (kreise ein) **T** (True) or **F** (False):

Moderator: Today I've got three <u>guests</u> in our studio who are going to talk about their personal <u>idols</u>. Tell us, Lucas, who is your personal <u>hero</u> or <u>heroine</u>?

Lucas: My personal hero is Mahatma Gandhi.

Moderator: Why is that?

Lucas: There are so many <u>reasons</u> why. He was such a <u>patient</u>, tolerant and <u>peaceful</u> man. He always told the <u>truth</u> and his life motto was <u>non-violence</u>. He was kind to animals and a <u>strict</u> <u>vegetarian</u>.

Moderator: Yes, he was a very <u>wise</u> man. And Ella, who is your idol?

Ella: <u>Amazing</u>! We are back to India because my heroine is Mother Teresa. I really <u>adore</u> her because she lived with the poor people in Calcutta and helped them. She gave them a home and the feeling that they were loved by somebody. She cared for <u>lepers</u> and other <u>terminally-ill</u> people and for children that had no parents. She gave her whole life to the poorest people in India and all over the world. She <u>received</u> the <u>Nobel Peace Prize</u> in 1979 and again she gave all the money to the poor. She was a real heroine. She was a saint.

Moderator: Yes she was. Thank you, Ella. And <u>last but not least</u>, my third guest. Leo, who is your personal idol?

Leo: My personal hero is our neighbour.

Moderator: That's interesting. Can you tell us why?

Leo: It's because he is <u>disabled</u> and has to sit in a <u>wheelchair</u> but he is such a friendly, <u>hopeful</u> and positive man. He lost both his legs in an accident. But he has never ever given up hope and he is full of <u>joy</u>. He is interested in what is going on around him and he has got lots of friends. He had to go through hard times when he couldn't work in his old job any longer. But <u>finally</u> he found a new job at our <u>local newspaper</u>. He is <u>brilliant</u> at writing stories and he helped me and my friends a lot with his articles when we were fighting for a new <u>playing field</u> in our town. It is always good to be with him.

Moderator: Thank you, Leo. Now we have to say goodbye to our listeners. Many thanks to our guests in the studio and please join us again next week.

guest	Gast	*leper*	Leprakranke / -r
idol	Idol / Vorbild	*terminally-ill*	todkrank
hero, heroine	Held, Heldin	*receive*	erhalten
reason	Grund	*Nobel Peace Prize*	Friedensnobelpreis
patient	geduldig	*last but not least*	nicht zuletzt
peaceful	friedlich	*disabled*	behindert
truth	Wahrheit	*wheelchair*	Rollstuhl
non-violence	Gewaltlosigkeit	*hopeful*	hoffnungsvoll
strict	streng	*joy*	Freude
vegetarian	Vegetarier	*finally*	schließlich
wise	weise	*local newspaper*	Lokalzeitung
amazing	erstaunlich	*brilliant*	hervorragend
adore	verehren	*playing field*	Spielplatz

1. F (three guests)
2. F (about their idols)
3. T
4. T
5. T
6. F (He was a strict vegetarian.)
7. T
8. F (Mother Teresa gave everyone the feeling to be loved.)
9. T
10. F (in 1979)
11. T
12. T
13. F (his legs)
14. T
15. F (After the accident he found a new job at the local newspaper.)
16. T

54 Listen to the interview with Megan talking about the place she would like to visit and **circle** (kreise ein) **T** (True) or **F** (False):

Reporter: Megan, which places would you like to visit?
Megan: I'd like to visit New Orleans one day. It's in the state of Louisiana, more <u>exactly</u> in the South-East and it is <u>situated</u> on the Mississippi River. You know, <u>I'm into</u> jazz and so I <u>definitely</u> have to go to the <u>birthplace</u> of jazz.
Reporter: Which <u>sights</u> would you like to see there?
Megan: The French Quarter.
Reporter: What is it <u>famous</u> for?
Megan: It's famous for its <u>street artists</u> and its bars with live music and its little restaurants. The food of New Orleans is famous. They serve ethnic food.
Reporter: What is ethnic food?
Megan: It is food that comes from <u>different</u> <u>cultural influences</u> and traditions. Let's say it is <u>multicultural</u> food.
Reporter: What else would you like to do in New Orleans?
Megan: I'd like to walk down Bourbon Street and visit Jackson Square and the French Market which is the oldest market in the United States. In the French Quarter you can find houses from the 19th <u>century</u> and many small shops and coffee bars.
Reporter: How do you know all these <u>facts</u>?
Megan: I saw a film about New Orleans and now I <u>absolutely</u> want to visit it. And <u>of course</u> I'd like to take a ride on the Mississippi River on a <u>steamboat</u>.
Reporter: Sounds great! What else can you do in New Orleans?
Megan: There are wonderful parks, nice botanical gardens, a zoo and an aquarium. And then the town is famous for its <u>numerous</u> festivals, like the Carnival and the many music festivals. There's not only jazz but also R&B, soul, gospel music, reggae, hip-hop and lots more.
Reporter: I remember there was a great <u>disaster</u> some years ago.
Megan: Yes, it was Hurricane Katrina in August 2005. It was a tropical <u>cyclone</u> which killed about 1500 people and <u>flooded</u> 80% of the city.
Reporter: Yes, it was an awful catastrophe.
Megan: But the town was <u>reconstructed</u>.
Reporter: I thank you for talking to me and I hope your dream of visiting New Orleans will come true one day.
Megan: It <u>surely</u> will.

exactly	genau	century	Jahrhundert
situated	gelegen	fact	Tatsache
be into	sehr mögen	absolutely	total
definitely	zweifellos	of course	natürlich
birthplace	Geburtsort	steamboat	Dampfschiff
sight	Sehenswürdigkeit	numerous	zahlreich
famous	berühmt	disaster	Katastrophe
street artist	Straßenkünstler	cyclone	Wirbelsturm
different	verschieden	flood	überfluten
cultural influence	Kultureinfluss	reconstruct	wieder errichten
multicultural	multikulturell	surely	sicherlich

1. F (in the South-East)
2. F (the birthplace of jazz)
3. F (She is into jazz.)
4. T
5. T
6. T
7. F (the oldest market)
8. F (19th century)
9. F (She saw a film.)
10. T
11. T
12. T
13. F (in 2005)
14. F (It killed about 1500 people.)
15. T
16. T

55 Listen to Molly calling her friend from Vienna and **circle** (kreise ein) **T** (True) or **F** (False):

Molly: Hi, Caroline! This is Molly speaking.
Caroline: Hi, Molly! How are you doing?
Molly: I'm doing fine! I'm on a holiday in Vienna.
Caroline: Great! Who is with you?
Molly: I'm here with my family. <u>Even</u> my grandparents are with us. I <u>mean</u> my father's parents. My mother's parents are too old. They didn't want to <u>join</u> us.
Caroline: Then you are a big group!
Molly: Yes, there are seven of us.
Caroline: What is the weather like in Austria?
Molly: It's <u>gorgeous</u>! It's been sunny all the time. No rain at all. And it's hot. Today it's 27 <u>degrees</u> Celsius.
Caroline: Sounds great! What have you been doing so far?
Molly: We have been visiting lots of sights like, for example, the Prater, where we took a ride on the famous <u>Giant Ferris Wheel</u>. We <u>enjoyed</u> a <u>breathtaking</u> <u>view</u> of Vienna from up there. We also visited Schönbrunn Castle, the <u>former</u> summer residence of the Habsburg <u>emperors</u> and <u>empresses</u>. I liked the park very much with its <u>fountains</u> and <u>statues</u>. Then it was <u>fascinating</u> to see the Orangery Garden and the Palm House. There was so much to see.
Caroline: How interesting! What did you like most?
Molly: That's difficult to say because there were so many <u>sights</u> I really liked. There was the Spanish Riding School, for example, with its <u>world-famous</u> Lippizaners. We watched the morning exercise of the horses. It was fantastic! Then I was really <u>impressed</u> by the Hundertwasser House: It is a really <u>crazy</u> house, very colourful and with green plants and trees on the <u>balconies</u> and on the roof. It looks wonderful! Then we visited St. Stephen's Cathedral which is the symbol of Vienna. It's a Gothic cathedral. I liked the <u>sound</u> of its bell, the "Pummerin" very much. So I really can't <u>decide</u> what I liked most. And Austrian food is very <u>tasty</u>!
Caroline: I see. Was there anything that you didn't like?
Molly: Yes, there was. What I found really <u>disgusting</u> was the <u>exhibition</u> about human bodies. It was so <u>gross</u>! I couldn't watch it. I had to wait for my family outside the museum.
Caroline: When you come back, you'll have to tell me more! What else are you going to visit?
Molly: We are going to visit the <u>Danube Tower</u> and we are planning on having dinner at the <u>rotating</u> restaurant on it. Dad has already booked a table for us. Then mum would like to visit the Albertina and see paintings of Klimt, Schiele and Picasso. And on our last day dad wants to go to Grinzing and <u>taste</u> the <u>famous</u> wine there. He wants to take some bottles back home.

Caroline: I'm looking forward to seeing all your photos.
Molly: Yes, we've taken over 300 pictures so far. There's so much to see in Vienna!
We <u>definitely</u> have to come back again next year.
Caroline: OK, Molly, have a nice time in Vienna. See you next week and thanks for calling.
Molly: See you!

even	sogar	*world-famous*	weltberühmt
mean	meinen	*impressed*	beeindruckt
join	mitkommen	*crazy*	verrückt
gorgeous	traumhaft	*balcony*	Balkon
degree	Grad	*sound*	Klang
Giant Ferris Wheel	Riesenrad	*decide*	sich entscheiden
enjoy	genießen	*tasty*	schmackhaft
breathtaking	atemberaubend	*disgusting*	abstoßend
view	Ausblick	*exhibition*	Ausstellung
former	früher / -e / -er / -es	*gross*	ekelhaft
emperor	Kaiser	*Danube Tower*	Donauturm
empress	Kaiserin	*rotating*	sich drehend
fountain	Brunnen	*taste*	kosten
statue	Statue	*famous*	berühmt
fascinating	faszinierend	*definitely*	auf jeden Fall
sight	Sehenswürdigkeit		

1. F (together with her family)
2. F (her mother's parents)
3. T
4. T
5. F (It was the former summer residence.)
6. T
7. F (the morning exercise)
8. T

9. F (St. Stephen's Cathedral)
10. F (She couldn't decide what she liked most.)
11. T
12. F (She found it disgusting.)
13. T
14. T
15. F (some bottles of wine)

56 Listen to Ethan talking about his dream holiday and **tick the correct answers**:

Interviewer: Hello Ethan. Welcome to our studio. Please tell us about your favourite place for a holiday.
Ethan: Well, the place where I would like to spend my holidays is in the <u>mountains</u>.
Interviewer: In the mountains? Isn't that a bit boring?
Ethan: I don't think so. You know, I'm not into swimming and lying on the beach all the time or reading in the sun. That's boring for me.
Interviewer: I see. What are you going to do in the mountains? Do you go mountain biking?
Ethan: No, I'd like to walk from <u>alpine hut</u> to alpine hut for about a week. That is what I call an <u>adventure</u>.
Interviewer: Sounds great! Who's going to <u>join</u> you?
Ethan: <u>Perhaps</u> my father and my elder brother. My mum and my sister are <u>afraid of</u> the mountains. My cousin has no time and my grandparents are too old.
Interviewer: What <u>equipment</u> do you need for such an adventure?
Ethan: Most important of all is a <u>rain jacket</u> and <u>of course</u> good <u>hiking boots</u> and warm clothes. Then, I always take my <u>walking sticks</u> with me, a helmet and a <u>rope</u> for <u>difficult</u> <u>passages</u> where you have to climb. And one can't <u>forget</u> to bring a warm <u>sleeping bag</u>. In the mountains it can be very cold at night, <u>even</u> in a hut. And <u>last but not least</u> I need my camera and a mobile phone <u>in order to</u> call for help <u>in case of</u> an <u>accident</u>.
Interviewer: Aren't you afraid of having no signal in the mountains?
Ethan: No, because the <u>emergency call</u> always works.
Interviewer: Do you also take something to eat or drink with you?
Ethan: Yes, that's <u>a must</u>. I always have a bottle of water, <u>dried fruits</u> and nuts with me. <u>Moreover</u>, you should take <u>bandages</u> and <u>dressing</u> with you in case of an emergency. You never know!

mountain	Berg	*forget*	vergessen
alpine hut	Berghütte	*sleeping bag*	Schlafsack
adventure	Abenteuer	*even*	sogar
join	begleiten	*last but not least*	nicht zuletzt
perhaps	vielleicht	*in order to*	um zu
be afraid of	sich fürchten	*in case of*	im Falle
equipment	Ausrüstung	*accident*	Unfall
rain jacket	Regenjacke	*emergency call*	Notruf
of course	natürlich	*a must*	ein Muss
hiking boots	Wanderschuhe	*dried fruits*	Trockenfrüchte
walking sticks	Wanderstöcke	*moreover*	außerdem
rope	Seil	*bandage*	Bandage / Verband
difficult	schwierig	*dressing*	Verbandszeug
passage	Passage / Stelle		

1. c
2. a
3. c
4. b
5. c
6. d

57 Listen to Rose talking about her dream holiday and **circle** (kreise ein) **T** (True) or **F** (False):

Interviewer: Hello Rose. May I ask you a few questions about your <u>dream</u> holiday for our school magazine?

Rose: Yes, <u>of course</u>. My dream holiday is to spend some weeks in the <u>desert</u> and live with a Berber family in the Sahara.

Interviewer: How amazing! Why is that?

Rose: I saw the film Lawrence of Arabia and there were really <u>breathtaking</u> <u>landscapes</u>. Then, I collected pictures of <u>huge</u> yellow and orange sand <u>dunes</u>. Some of them are <u>nearly</u> 200m high. The desert is so fascinating and I would like to sleep under the stars and meet <u>nomadic people</u>. I'd like to take a camel ride at <u>sunrise</u> in <u>silvery</u> light. It's also <u>possible</u> to <u>rent</u> a jeep with <u>four-wheel drive</u>. I want to <u>experience</u> everything.

Interviewer: How interesting. But isn't it very hot in the desert? The <u>heat</u> during the day must be brutal.

Rose: Yes, it is and there is no <u>shade</u>, so you have to <u>cover</u> your head but at night it is very cold. However, it must be great to go camping out under the stars.

Interviewer: Aren't you afraid of the dark?

Rose: No, I like the <u>challenge</u>.

Interviewer: And what about sandstorms? Aren't they very dangerous?

Rose: Yes, they are but you see them coming. Far away the air <u>turns yellow</u> but you have got enough time to get into your car, to go to a <u>shelter</u> or to go into a <u>tent</u>. There you can <u>enjoy</u> a nice glass of sweet <u>mint</u> tea and wait until the storm is over.

Interviewer: I am sure a holiday in the desert will be a great <u>adventure</u>. You have to be very fit, don't you?

Rose: Yes, you are right because walking through the sand is <u>tough</u> and the heat is <u>exhausting</u>. <u>Moreover</u>, you must be careful not to <u>drop</u> anything small onto the sand because you won't find it again. And of course the <u>powdery</u> sand goes everywhere: into your socks, into your <u>underwear</u>, into your mouth, but that <u>doesn't matter</u>. The desert is a highlight. An oasis with <u>palm trees</u> and a little <u>pond</u> is a second highlight.

Interviewer: Then, Rose, I hope that your dream will come true one day.

Rose: Thank you very much.

dream	Traum	*cover*	bedecken
of course	natürlich	*challenge*	Herausforderung
desert	Wüste	*turn yellow*	gelb werden
breathtaking	atemberaubend	*shelter*	Schutz
landscape	Landschaft	*tent*	Zelt
huge	sehr groß	*enjoy*	genießen
dune	Düne	*mint*	Minze
nearly	fast	*adventure*	Abenteuer
nomadic people	Nomaden	*tough*	zäh / hart
sunrise	Sonnenaufgang	*exhausting*	beschwerlich
silvery	silbern	*moreover*	außerdem
possible	möglich	*drop*	fallen lassen
rent	mieten	*powdery*	pudrig
four-wheel drive	Allradantrieb	*underwear*	Unterwäsche
experience	erleben	*it doesn't matter*	es macht nichts aus
heat	Hitze	*palm tree*	Palme
shade	Schatten	*pond*	Teich

1. T
2. T
3. F (yellow and orange)
4. F (at sunrise)
5. T

6. F (The heat is brutal.)
7. T
8. F (It is tough.)
9. T
10. T

58 Listen to the radio programme *Breakfast All over the World* and **fill in the missing words:**

Moderator: Welcome to our phone-in programme. Today we are going to talk about our <u>callers'</u> favourite breakfasts. The first caller is Will from Dublin. Hello Will.

Will: Hello to everybody. Well, my favourite breakfast is <u>porridge</u> with <u>cream</u> or milk with a bit of salt and <u>loads of</u> brown sugar. I also like <u>bacon</u> and eggs together with <u>fried</u> <u>mushrooms</u> and tomatoes. Or, I eat fried <u>thin</u> <u>sausages</u> with ketchup or Worcester sauce. Before I <u>fry</u> the sausages, I always make a little <u>hole</u> in the sausages so that they don't explode. On Sundays I'm very <u>fond of</u> baked beans on toast. I sometimes have <u>black pudding</u> with <u>potato bread</u>. Yes, that's all.

Moderator: Thank you for calling, Will. And next <u>on the line</u> is Elena from Mexico. Hi, Elena.

Elena: Hi, this is Elena calling from Merida. I love to eat tortillas with rice, beans and eggs in a <u>spicy</u> red sauce. On Sundays I sometimes have a <u>seafood</u> cocktail, again with a very <u>hot</u> sauce. Of course I like bacon and eggs with beans and <u>pickled</u> onions. I always finish my breakfast with sweet cake sticks, which I dip in thick, hot chocolate. That's <u>tasty</u>!

Moderator: Thank you Elena and goodbye! Our last caller for today is Anila from India. Good evening, Anila.

Anila: Hi, I'm calling from Delhi. I only eat fruits in the morning: grapes, mangos, bananas, <u>figs</u>, oranges and many more. My brother <u>prefers</u> <u>curry</u> in the morning. He says he needs something <u>filling</u>. Then he likes <u>pancakes</u> with vegetables or <u>crispy</u> potatoes with eggs. He sometimes eats rice with <u>lentils</u>. Goodbye from India.

Moderator: Goodbye to our callers and to our listeners. <u>Join</u> me again next Friday.

caller	Anrufer	*on the line*	in der Leitung
porridge	Haferbrei	*spicy*	scharf / pikant
cream	Rahm / Schlagsahne	*seafood*	Meeresfrüchte
loads of	viel	*hot*	scharf
bacon	Speck	*pickled*	in Essig eingelegt
fried	gebraten	*tasty*	lecker / schmackhaft
mushroom	Pilz	*fig*	Feige
thin	dünn	*prefer*	vorziehen
sausage	Wurst	*curry*	Eintopfgericht (Indien)
fry	braten	*filling*	sättigend
hole	Loch	*pancake*	Palatschinke / Pfannkuchen
to be fond of	sehr gerne mögen	*crispy*	knusprig
black pudding	Blutwurst	*lentil*	Linse
potato bread	Fladenbrot aus Kartoffelmehl	*join*	dabei sein

1. Will's favourite breakfast is **porridge** with **cream** or milk and **loads / lots / a lot** of brown sugar.
2. He also likes **bacon** and eggs with **fried** mushrooms and **tomatoes**.
3. He also eats fried thin **sausages** with ketchup or Worcester sauce.
4. Before he fries the sausages, he always makes a little **hole** in the sausages so that they don't **explode**.
5. On Sundays he is **fond** of baked **beans** on toast.
6. Will sometimes has black **pudding** with potato **bread**.
7. Elena from Mexico loves tortillas with **spicy / hot** red sauce.
8. The tortillas are filled with **rice**, **beans** and eggs.
9. On Sundays she sometimes has a **seafood** cocktail with a very **spicy / hot** sauce.
10. She also likes bacon and eggs with **beans** and pickled **onions**.
11. She loves to **dip** sweet cake sticks in thick, hot **chocolate**.
12. Anila from Delhi only eats **fruits** in the morning like **grapes**, **mango(e)s**, bananas, **figs** and oranges.
13. Her brother prefers **curry / curries** in the morning because he needs something **filling**.
14. He also has **pancakes** with **vegetables** or crispy **potatoes** with eggs.
15. He also likes rice with **lentils**.

59 Listen to the radio programme *Breakfast All over the World* and **tick** (kreuze an) **the correct answers:**

Moderator: Welcome again to our phone-in programme *Breakfast All over the World*. Today we are going to talk to people from Sweden, France and the Philippines. Our first <u>caller</u> is Elsa from Stockholm, Sweden. Hello Elsa.

Elsa: Hello to everybody. Well, I love sandwiches in the morning. I like to <u>top</u> them with butter, cheese, <u>peppers</u>, <u>cucumbers</u> or tomatoes. Our bread is <u>slightly</u> sweet. But we also have <u>crisp bread</u> and I love to <u>spread</u> <u>liver paté</u> on it and eat it with <u>pickles</u>. I'm also <u>fond of</u> <u>smoked salmon</u>. On Sundays I sometimes eat a hard or <u>soft boiled egg</u> with caviar on top of it. That's great! And I really like muesli with yoghurt mixed with nuts and <u>dried fruit</u>.

Moderator: Thank you for calling, Elsa. And next <u>on the line</u> is Pierre from France. Welcome to our programme, Pierre.

Pierre: Good evening! I'm calling from Paris. What I like most about my breakfast is, <u>of course</u>, our croissants. I usually <u>dip</u> them in my bowl of coffee with milk. But I also love baguettes with jam and butter or bread rolls with chocolate <u>filling</u> on a Sunday morning. I like orange juice or freshly <u>sliced</u> fruits. I sometimes eat a bowl of yoghurt and in the summer, when it's very hot, I love to eat a bowl of ice cream.

Moderator: Thank you, Pierre. And our last caller is Danilo from the Philippines.

Danilo: Hello to everybody. My favourite breakfast is <u>tamales</u>. They are made from <u>rice flour</u> and are filled with chicken and sometimes we also put <u>duck</u> eggs into them. Then we <u>wrap</u> the tamales in banana <u>leaves</u> and then they are cooked. Of course, we don't eat the banana leaves. Tamales are really tasty and I eat them every morning. They are filling and I'm not hungry until the evening.

Moderator: Thanks for calling, Danilo. <u>Unfortunately</u>, time is up again. But please <u>join</u> me again next Friday at the <u>same time</u>.

caller	Lieblings-	*on the line*	in der Leitung
top	Brot belegen	*of course*	natürlich
pepper	Paprika	*dip*	eintauchen
cucumber	Gurke	*filling*	Füllung
slightly	leicht / ein bisschen	*sliced*	geschnitten
crisp bread	Knäckebrot	*tamale*	gefüllte Reismehltasche
spread	bestreichen	*rice flour*	Reismehl
liver paté	Leberpastete	*duck*	Ente
pickles	eingelegtes Gemüse	*wrap*	einwickeln
be fond of	sehr gerne haben	*leaf, leaves*	Blatt, Blätter
smoked salmon	Räucherlachs	*unfortunately*	unglücklicherweise
soft boiled egg	weiches Ei	*join*	dabei sein
dried fruit	Trockenfrüchte	*same time*	selbe Zeit

1.	d		5.	d
2.	c		6.	b
3.	a		7.	a
4.	c		8.	d

60 Listen to the radio programme *Breakfast All over the World* and **tick** (kreuze an) **the answers that are NOT correct**:

Moderator: It's Friday again. Welcome to our phone-in programme *Breakfast All over the World*. Today we are going to have three <u>callers</u> from Morocco, Vietnam and Japan. Now, let me see, who is first <u>on the line</u>? It's Husain from Morocco. Hello, Husein!

Husain: Hello to all the <u>listeners</u>! I'm calling from Casablanca. Well, I like French <u>pastries</u> for breakfast but I'm also <u>fond of</u> <u>pancakes</u> and cakes made from <u>semolina</u>. I love to eat my pancakes with butter, honey or jam made from <u>strawberries</u> or <u>apricots</u>. We also have many <u>kinds</u> of bread. Sometimes my grandma prepares a nice dip-sauce made from <u>almonds</u>, honey and oil. We dip our bread into this sauce. It tastes <u>delicious</u>! At the weekend we often have <u>goat</u>'s cheese, black olives and <u>fried</u> eggs. I sometimes have <u>dates</u> and <u>sliced</u> oranges. And we always have green tea with <u>mint</u> <u>leaves</u> and <u>loads of</u> sugar. And there is no breakfast for me without freshly pressed orange juice. Goodbye to all of you.

Moderator: Goodbye, Husein and our next call is from Hanoi. Thank you, Kai, for calling.

Khai: Hello to everyone! My breakfast is totally <u>different</u>! I really love soup in the morning. It's soup with <u>beef</u> or chicken and <u>rice noodles</u>, lemon and chilly. We call it Pho. I sometimes eat <u>crab</u> meat soup or noodles with <u>pork</u> and <u>herbs</u>. When there is more time left in the morning I <u>prepare</u> myself rice porridge with meat, fish or duck, or something sweet like an omelette with fried bananas. My best <u>regards</u> to all the listeners!

Moderator: Thank you Kai. And our last caller comes from Japan. Hello, Yuna!

Yuna: Hello from Japan! My favourite breakfast is fried rice omelette or coconut milk rice. It's really <u>tasty</u> and you can prepare it very <u>quickly</u>. If there's not much time, I make myself a <u>multi-grain</u> <u>shake</u> the evening before and the next morning I drink it while <u>getting dressed</u>.
Many <u>greetings</u> to all the listeners and <u>sayonara</u>!

caller	Anrufer	*leaf, leaves*	Blatt, Blätter
on the line	in der Leitung	*loads of*	viel
listener	Zuhörer	*different*	verschieden
pastry, pastries	Gebäck	*beef*	Rindfleisch
be fond of	gerne haben	*rice noodles*	Reisnudeln
pancake	Palatschinke / Pfannkuchen	*crab*	Krabbe
semolina	Grieß	*pork*	Schweinefleisch
strawberry	Erdbeere	*herbs*	Kräuter
apricot	Marille / Aprikose	*prepare*	zubereiten
kind	Art	*regards*	Grüße
almond	Mandel	*tasty*	schmackhaft
delicious	köstlich	*quick / -ly*	schnell
goat	Ziege	*multi-grain*	Mehrkorn
fried	gebraten	*shake*	Mixgetränk
date	Dattel	*get dressed*	sich anziehen
sliced	geschnitten	*greeting*	Gruß
mint	Minze	*sayonara*	japanisch: auf Wiedersehen

1.	d		3.	d
2.	b		4.	d

61 Listen to the radio programme about disasters and **circle** (kreise ein) **T** (True) or **F** (False):

Moderator: Welcome to *Lucky Coincidence*, our weekly programme about people who <u>escaped</u> a great <u>danger</u> <u>by chance</u>. Today my <u>guest</u> is Tom. Hello, Tom!

Tom: Hello and thank you for <u>inviting</u> me to the studio!

Moderator: Tell us what happened to you in summer 2017.
Tom: Well, my girlfriend Anna and I had a wonderful holiday in Portugal. We <u>rented</u> a car and drove around. In our third week we stayed at a small <u>bed & breakfast</u> in Pedrógão Grande in Central Portugal. We took long walks in the woods and enjoyed fresh <u>smell</u> of the <u>eucalyptus</u> trees. We were planning on staying for four days but on the third day I became <u>kind of</u> nervous. I thought it was because of the <u>enormous</u> <u>heat</u>. I absolutely wanted to leave one day earlier <u>even though</u> we had already paid for the b&b for four days. I wanted to go down to the beach in Faro. And that was what we did. The beach was great. At the sea it wasn't so hot any more. We were lying in the sand, reading and <u>relaxing</u> when I got a call from my parents. They were greatly <u>troubled</u> because around Pedrógão Grande a big <u>forest fire</u> had broken out. Hundreds of <u>firefighters</u> were fighting against the flames. Many small <u>villages</u> were <u>trapped</u> in the fire and many people died in their cars when they were trying to <u>flee</u> from the flames. They could not escape. The heavy storms started the fires and the flames <u>spread</u> very fast. Fallen trees <u>blocked</u> the roads, so it was nearly impossible for the <u>rescue teams</u> to <u>reach</u> the <u>victims</u> <u>in time</u>. Telephone lines were <u>destroyed</u> and there was <u>smoke</u> everywhere. The photos in the newspaper were horrible. We didn't <u>enjoy</u> the last week of our holiday any more. But <u>luckily</u> we were <u>safe</u> because an <u>inner voice</u> had told me to leave.
Moderator: Thank you Tom for telling your story.
Tom: <u>You're welcome</u>.

coincidence	Zufall	*firefighter*	Feuerwehrmann / - frau
escape	entkommen	*village*	Dorf
danger	Gefahr	*trapped*	gefangen / in der Falle
by chance	zufällig	*flee*	flüchten
guest	Gast	*spread, spread*	ausbreiten, breitete aus
invite	einladen	*block*	versperren / blockieren
rent	mieten	*rescue team*	Rettungsmannschaft
bed & breakfast	Pension	*reach*	erreichen
smell	Geruch	*victim*	Opfer
eucalyptus	Eukalyptus	*in time*	rechtzeitig
kind of	irgendwie	*destroy*	zerstören
enormous	riesig	*smoke*	Rauch
heat	Hitze	*enjoy*	genießen
even though	obwohl	*luckily*	glücklicherweise
relax	sich erholen	*safe*	in Sicherheit
troubled	beunruhigt	*inner voice*	innere Stimme
forest fire	Waldbrand	*You're welcome.*	Gern geschehen.

1. T
2. F (car)
3. T
4. T
5. T
6. T

7. F (many small villages)
8. T
9. T
10. T
11. F (An inner voice had told him to leave.)

62 Listen to a <u>mountain guide</u> and **circle** (kreise ein) **T** (True) or **F** (False):

Mountain guide: <u>It's a pity</u> that some tourists are really <u>unreasonable</u>.
Reporter: Please tell us what <u>happened</u> exactly the day before yesterday.
Mountain guide: Well, nine tourists had <u>booked</u> a tour with me in an <u>off-course area</u>. Early in the morning we climbed up the mountain on our <u>touring skis</u>. We started in fine weather. But suddenly, the weather changed, <u>clouds</u> came up and snowfall <u>set in</u>. I <u>broke off</u> the tour because I got an <u>avalanche</u> <u>warning</u> on my mobile phone. I told the group about it but some of them absolutely wanted to go down the <u>off-path</u> <u>slope</u>. I <u>advised</u> them, warned them and <u>finally</u> <u>ordered</u> them to <u>return</u> and go down the <u>safe</u> slope with me. Three tourists were <u>reasonable</u> and followed me. The others went down the <u>off-trail</u> slope <u>on their own</u>. The snowfall was so heavy by then that we couldn't see more

than two meters. It was even difficult to go down the safe slope. <u>Suddenly</u> we heard a loud <u>noise</u> like <u>thunder</u>. I knew what had happened and phoned the <u>rescue team</u>. Later they told me that a large wall of ice and snow had broken off the mountain and the avalanche <u>tumbled down</u> into the <u>valley</u>. One man was able to <u>free</u> himself from the <u>masses of snow</u>. He was only <u>slightly injured</u>. The others were <u>buried</u> under 5 metres of snow and ice.

Reporter: When did the rescue team arrive?

Mountain guide: It didn't <u>take long</u>. The mountain rescue team tried to find the skiers and looked for them with dogs and <u>sensors</u> but they were found dead <u>except for</u> the man who had freed himself.

Reporter: Thank you for the interview.

Mountain guide: You're welcome.

mountain guide	Bergführer	*safe*	sicher
it's a pity	es ist schade	*reasonable*	vernünftig
unreasonable	unvernünftig	*off-trail*	abseits der Piste
happen	geschehen	*on their own*	alleine
book	buchen	*suddenly*	plötzlich
off-course area	Gelände abseits der Piste	*noise*	Lärm
touring ski	Tourenschi	*thunder*	Donner
cloud	Wolke	*rescue team*	Rettungsmannschaft
set in	einsetzen, setzte ein	*tumble down*	hinunterstürzen
break off, broke off	abbrechen, brach ab	*valley*	Tal
avalanche	Lawine	*free*	sich befreien
warning	Warnung	*masses of snow*	Schneemassen
off-path	abseits der Piste	*slightly injured*	leicht verletzt
slope	Hang	*buried*	begraben
advise	raten	*take long*	lange dauern
finally	schließlich	*sensor*	Sonde
order	befehlen	*except for*	außer
return	zurückkehren		

1. T
2. T
3. F (The mountain guide broke off the tour.)
4. T
5. F (three tourists)
6. F (The snowfall was very heavy.)
7. F (He didn't see it, he heard it. The rescue team told him about it later.)
8. F (He phoned the mountain rescue.)
9. T
10. F (One man could free himself.)

63 Listen to Mr Lopez talking about an earthquake and **circle** (kreise ein) **T** (True) or **F** (False):

Reporter: Mr Miguel Lopez <u>survived</u> the <u>powerful earthquake</u> in Mexico. Mr Lopez, can you please inform us what <u>happened</u> to you in September 2017?

Mr Lopez: Well, when I heard the alarm <u>siren</u> I <u>rushed</u> down into the <u>cellar</u> of my house and <u>hid</u> under a <u>door frame</u>. Then, I felt the ground <u>tremble</u> and <u>shake</u>. The shaking <u>lasted</u> for about 30 seconds and that was a long time. I heard walls <u>burst apart</u> and soon I was <u>covered</u> in <u>dust</u> and broken <u>bricks</u>. I heard cries from <u>neighbouring</u> houses and I started to <u>scream</u>, too because I couldn't get out of my <u>prison</u>. I was <u>trapped</u> under a big block of <u>concrete</u> and I felt great <u>pain</u> in my legs. But I <u>was lucky</u>. I had enough <u>air</u> to <u>breathe</u> and I could see the sky <u>above</u> me. My house was gone. It had <u>collapsed</u>.

Reporter: How long did you have to wait until <u>rescue</u> came?

Mr Lopez: I don't know exactly. <u>Maybe</u> two or three hours. Maybe more. The <u>worst</u> was that the earth did not stop shaking. There were lots of <u>minor</u> earthquakes and I really panicked. Then, I heard a dog <u>bark</u>. I screamed again. And then I saw a <u>search dog</u> with a bottle of water hanging from his neck. I <u>managed</u> to take the bottle with one hand, opened it with trembling fingers, and drank. It was the best water I had ever drunk in my life. I <u>guess</u> it took another three hours until I was <u>freed</u> from my prison. And it took a long time until I could be taken to a building that had not collapsed. Both my legs were broken and I had lost everything but I was so happy that I had survived.

Reporter: Is your family <u>safe</u>?

Mr Lopez: Yes, they are. It was like a <u>miracle</u>. My family was by the coast when the earthquake <u>destroyed</u> our home. They had wanted to come home earlier but my son had broken his arm and so they couldn't <u>return</u>.

Reporter: So that <u>bad luck</u> <u>turned out</u> to be <u>good luck</u> <u>in the end</u>!

Mr Lopez: Exactly.

survive	überleben	*air*	Luft
powerful	gewaltig	*breathe*	atmen
earthquake	Erdbeben	*above*	über
happen	passieren	*collapse*	zusammenfallen
siren	Sirene	*rescue*	Rettung
rush	stürzen	*maybe*	vielleicht
cellar	Keller	*worst*	am schlimmsten
hide, hid	verstecken, versteckte	*minor*	kleiner
door frame	Türstock	*panic, panicked*	in Panik greaten, geriet in P.
tremble	beben	*bark*	bellen
shake	zittern / schwanken	*search dog*	Rettungshund / Suchhund
last	dauern	*manage*	es schaffen
burst apart	zerbersten	*guess*	raten
covered	bedeckt	*freed*	befreit
dust	Staub	*safe*	in Sicherheit
brick	Ziegel	*miracle*	Wunder
neighbouring	benachbart	*destroy*	zerstören
scream	schreien	*return*	zurückkehren
prison	Gefängnis	*bad luck*	Pech
trapped	gefangen	*turn out*	ausfallen / sich herausstellen
concrete	Beton	*good luck*	Glück
pain	Schmerz	*in the end*	schließlich
be lucky	Glück haben		

1. T
2. F (seconds)
3. T
4. T
5. T
6. T
7. F (to a building that had not collapsed)
8 F (not his arm)
9. T
10. T

64 Listen to the conversation about Hurricane Maria and **tick** (kreuze an) **the correct answers:**

Man: Did you watch <u>the news</u> about Hurricane Maria last week?

Woman: Yes, I watched them every day. The hurricane <u>struck</u> Puerto Rico at a <u>speed</u> of up to 280 km/h. <u>Imagine</u> that speed!

Man: It's really hard to <u>believe</u>! It <u>left</u> a <u>path</u> of <u>destruction</u> all over the country. It totally <u>destroyed</u> most of the towns.

Woman: Trees were <u>uprooted</u> and those that were still <u>upright</u> had lost all their <u>leaves</u>. It looked <u>spooky</u>.

Man: Yes, I saw the picture in the newspaper.

Woman: All the banana plantations were destroyed.

Man: I know. <u>Moreover</u>, many roads were <u>flooded</u> and had to be closed because of heavy rainfall.

Woman: The hurricane blew everything away: roofs, walls, doors, windows, cars and <u>cattle</u>.

Man: But the <u>worst</u> thing is that many people died under fallen trees or <u>concrete</u>. Most of them died of <u>heart attacks</u>, in <u>accidents</u> or in <u>flood waters</u>. And there are still lots of people <u>missing</u>.

Woman: Horrible! Many <u>injured</u> people couldn't be <u>rescued</u> because <u>car wrecks</u>, <u>mudslides</u>, trees and rocks <u>blocked</u> the roads. And many roads were simply <u>washed away</u>.

Man: Yes, and there was no <u>electricity</u> for a long time, no TV, no radio or Internet, so Puerto Rico was totally <u>cut off.</u>

Woman: In some <u>parts</u> of the country there is still no electricity. And people have no food or fresh water.

Man: The <u>intensity</u> of hurricanes has <u>increased</u> over the last years and I am sure that this is because of <u>climate change</u>. The ocean temperatures become higher and this <u>means</u> heavier storms.

Woman: You're absolutely right.

the news	die Nachrichten	*heart attack*	Herzanfall
strike, struck	treffen, traf	*accident*	Unfall
speed	Geschwindigkeit	*flood water*	Hochwasser
imagine	sich vorstellen	*missing*	vermisst
believe	glauben	*injured*	verletzt
leave, left	hinterlassen, hinterließ	*rescued*	gerettet
path	Weg / Pfad	*car wreck*	Autowrack
destruction	Zerstörung	*mudslide*	Mure
destroy	zerstören	*block*	versperren
uproot	entwurzeln	*washed away*	weggeschwemmt
upright	aufrecht	*electricity*	Elektrizität
leaf, leaves	Blatt, Blätter	*cut off*	abgeschnitten
spooky	gespenstisch	*part*	Teil
moreover	außerdem	*intensity*	Heftigkeit
flooded	überflutet	*increase*	zunehmen
cattle	Vieh	*climate change*	Klimawandel
worst	am schlimmsten	*mean*	bedeuten
concrete	Beton		

1.	c	4.	b
2.	d	5.	c
3.	a	6.	d

65 Listen to Ella talking about a TV programme about volcanic eruptions and **fill in the missing words:**

Ella: I saw an interesting <u>report</u> on TV yesterday.
Adam: What was it about?
Ella: It was about <u>volcanic eruptions</u>.
Adam: Was it on the Science Channel at 6 pm?
Ella: Yes, <u>exactly</u>.
Adam: I <u>normally</u> watch it, too. But yesterday we weren't at home.
Ella: They showed <u>terrific</u> pictures in <u>slow motion</u> of a volcano <u>spewing</u> fire and smoke. And then <u>lava</u> was slowly running down the mountain <u>covering</u> everything: woods, fields and houses.
Adam: Were people <u>injured</u> or killed?
Ella: No, <u>fortunately</u> not. <u>Scientists</u> knew that there would be an eruption and so people and <u>cattle</u> could be <u>evacuated</u> before the <u>disaster</u>. Before the <u>outbreak</u> they could <u>measure</u> small <u>earthquakes</u> on the <u>Richter scale</u>. Then birds flew away and everything went <u>silent</u>. And suddenly, with an <u>enormous</u> <u>thundering sound</u>, a big <u>cloud</u> of <u>ash</u> and gases was blown into the air followed by red <u>magma</u>. The sun <u>darkened</u> from the volcanic ash. My dad <u>recorded</u> the programme, so you can come round and watch it for yourself whenever you want to.
Adam: That would be great! Thank you!

report	Bericht	*disaster*	Katastrophe
volcanic eruption	Vulkanausbruch	*outbreak*	Ausbruch
exactly	genau	*measure*	messen
normally	normalerweise	*earthquake*	Erdbeben
terrific	sagenhaft	*Richter scale*	Richter Skala
slow motion	Zeitlupe	*silent*	still
spew	speien	*enormous*	enorm / gewaltig
lava	Lava	*thundering*	donnernd
cover	bedecken	*sound*	Laut / Geräusch
injured	verletzt	*cloud*	Wolke
fortunately	glücklicherweise	*ash*	Asche
scientist	Wissenschafter	*magma*	Magma / flüssiges Gestein
cattle	Vieh	*darken*	verdunkeln
evacuated	evakuiert / umgesiedelt	*record*	aufnehmen

1. The report on TV was about **volcanic eruptions**.
2. Adam **normally** watches the programme but he was not at home that evening.
3. They showed **terrific** pictures in slow **motion**.

4. A volcano spewed **fire** and **smoke**.
5. The lava was **running** down the mountain **covering** everything.
6. People and cattle could be **evacuated** before the **disaster / catastrophe**.
7. Small **earthquakes** could be **measured** on the Richter scale.
8. Before the outbreak everything was **silent / quiet** and the birds flew away.
9. Then, with an enormous **thundering sound,** a big cloud of ash and **gases** was sent into the air.
10. Red **magma / lava** ran down the mountain.
11. The sun darkened from the volcanic **ash**.

66 Listen to the news and **match** (füge zusammen) **the sentence halves** (die Satzhälften):

Good evening, Ladies and Gentlemen. This is Collin Brown speaking. This is the latest news for today. Central Europe has been facing the worst floods ever. The floods have claimed more than 90 victims. In a camping site many tourists saw their cars and tents being washed out into the sea. Rescue teams, volunteers and soldiers have been filling sandbags with tons of sand and building high walls with them. Cities are underwater because dams have broken. Residents were evacuated before the floods came. Rivers had to be closed to all ships. Roads were impassable because they had been washed out. And because the heavy rain won't stop for the next few days there is a high danger of mudslides coming down the mountains. That is not the only damage but there is another economic catastrophe: tourists have cancelled their holidays and that means a disaster for all tourist destinations.
And now the weather for tomorrow: It's heavy rain again in the morning letting up towards the afternoon. This has been the latest news. Goodbye to all our listeners.

latest news	neueste Nachrichten	resident	Bewohner
face	begegnen / sich stellen	evacuated	evakuiert / umgesiedelt
flood	Flut / Überschwemmung	impassable	unpassierbar
claim	fordern	danger	Gefahr
victim	Opfer	mudslide	Mure
site	Anlage / Platz	damage	Schaden
tent	Zelt	economic	wirtschaftlich
washed out	weggeschwemmt	catastrophe	Katastrophe
rescue team	Rettungsmannschaft	cancel	absagen / stornieren
volunteer	Freiwilliger	disaster	Katastrophe
soldier	Soldat	destination	Reiseziel
sandbag	Sandsack	let up	nachlassen
dam	Damm	listener	Zuhörer

1. e
2. g
3. i
4. j
5. a
6. b
7. c
8. d
9. f
10. h

67 Listen to a girl trapped in a snowstorm and **tick** (kreuze an) **the correct answers:**

Mountain Rescue: Hello, Mountain Rescue.
Girl: We are trapped in a snowstorm.
Mountain Rescue: How many of you are there?
Girl: There's four of us.
Mountain Rescue: Is anybody hurt?
Girl: No, we are all OK.
Mountain Rescue: Where are you exactly?
Girl: We were on our way to Eagle's Peak. We've walked for about one and a half hours. We started in fine weather but now the weather has changed. We have already looked for an alpine hut but there aren't any. What shall we do?
Mountain Rescue: Stay where you are and put on all the clothes you have got with you. Then, huddle together and eat all the food you have taken with you. While waiting

for us sing songs, tell stories, but do not <u>fall asleep</u>. Rescue will be with you in about 30 minutes. The rescue team has already started running up the mountain, and you can call any time you want. I'll be here for you.

Girl: Thank you so much.

Mountain Rescue	Bergrettung	*alpine hut*	Berghütte
trapped	gefangen / in der Falle sein	*shall*	sollen
hurt	verletzt	*huddle together*	sich zusammendrängen
exactly	genau	*fall asleep*	einschlafen
Eagle's Peak	Adlerspitze		

1.   b   3.   a
2.   c   4.   c

68   Listen to the interview about the <u>impacts</u> of a <u>drought</u> and **circle** (kreise ein) **T** (True) or **F** (False):

Moderator: In today's programme we are going to talk about the dangers a drought can <u>bring about</u>. In our studio we welcome Mr Lucas Turner, an expert on <u>natural disasters</u>. Mr Turner, what will happen if there is no rain in a <u>certain</u> <u>area</u> for more than half a year?

Mr Turner: It <u>depends on</u> the region. If there is enough water in a <u>nearby</u> lake or in a river and if the climate is not too hot, the <u>damage</u> will be small. But if a <u>period</u> of <u>dry</u> weather <u>lasts</u> for many months in a very hot region, <u>crops</u> and plants will <u>suffer</u> great damage. They will <u>dry up</u>. <u>Consequences</u> of drought may even be <u>famine</u> because people can't <u>grow</u> vegetables or <u>farm</u> animals without water. Another impact is <u>poverty</u>.

Moderator: I see. If there is no water, there are no crops and no <u>income</u>.

Mr Turner: Exactly. A drought may also bring about <u>forest fires</u>. But the <u>worst</u> impact of a drought is that animals and people die.

Moderator: Mr Turner, you are a <u>member</u> of *HAP*. What does *HAP* mean?

Mr Turner: It means *Help for African People*. We try to help African people because they are really <u>threatened</u> by drought. In Africa, for example, people have to walk for miles to find a <u>water hole</u>. Then they have to carry the water back to their village. This is <u>mainly</u> done by women and children, so most children don't go to school which again <u>leads</u> to poverty.

Moderator: Is there anything we can do for the people in Africa?

Mr Turner: Yes, there is. You can <u>donate</u> money to <u>volunteer</u> organisations like *HAP* and many more that look for water and build <u>wells</u> or schools, for example.

Moderator: Thank you, Mr Turner.

Mr Turner: <u>Thanks for having me.</u>

impact	Auswirkung	*famine*	Hungersnot
drought	Trockenheit / Dürre	*grow*	anbauen
bring about	mit sich bringen	*farm*	züchten
natural disaster	Naturkatastrophe	*poverty*	Armut
certain	bestimmt	*income*	Einkommen
area	Gebiet	*forest fire*	Waldbrand
depend on	abhängen von	*worst*	schlimmste / -r / -s
nearby	nahegelegen	*member*	Mitglied
damage	Schaden	*threatened*	bedroht
period	Periode	*water hole*	Wasserloch
dry	trocken	*mainly*	hauptsächlich
last	andauern	*lead*	führen
crop	Ernte / Ertrag	*donate*	spenden
suffer	erleiden	*volunteer*	freiwillig
dry up	vertrocknen	*well*	Brunnen
consequence	Folge	*Thanks for having me.*	Danke für die Einladung.

1.   T   4.   F (A drought may bring about forest fires.)
2.   T   5.   F (that people die)
3.   T   6.   F (Help for African People)

7. F (they walk)
8 F (by women and children)

9. F (Most children don't go to school.)
10. T

69 Listen to Mrs Harper talking about tsunamis and **circle** (kreise ein) **T** (True) or **F** (False):

Moderator: In today's programme *The World's Greatest Disasters* we are going to talk about tsunamis. We welcome Rachel Harper from the meteorological institute. Good evening, Mrs Harper.

Mrs Harper: Good evening.

Moderator: Perhaps you could explain to our listeners what exactly a tsunami is.

Mrs Harper: Of course. A tsunami can be a series of waves that travel very quickly or it can also be one single, giant wave up to 30 metres high that rushes towards the coast. The waves can travel very long distances.

Moderator: Are tsunamis always that high?

Mrs Harper: No, out in the open ocean they are small but near the coast they pile up high.

Moderator: What causes a tsunami?

Mrs Harper: A tsunami may be caused by earthquakes deep down in the ocean, by a volcanic eruption in the sea or by landslides deep down in the water.

Moderator: Is the name "killer wave" justified?

Mrs Harper: Yes, they really are killer waves because they are so powerful and strong that they destroy everything: villages on the coast, forests of palm trees, really everything.

Moderator: Are there no warning signs before a tsunami arrives at the coast?

Mrs Harper: Yes, there may be some signs. There might be, for example, an earthquake. But not all earthquakes create a tsunami. Sometimes the water withdraws far away from the coast only to come back as a killer wave a few minutes later. But there are also tsunamis that arrive unexpectedly. And that is why people living on the coast or tourists at the beach might be surprised by the deadly wave. When the wave hits the coast, escape is nearly impossible because you can't run away from a tsunami.

Moderator: Thank you, Mrs Harper, for your information.

Mrs Harper: You're welcome.

meteorological	meteorologisch / Wetter-	*volcanic eruption*	Vulkanausbruch
perhaps	vielleicht	*landslide*	Erdrutsch
exactly	genau	*justified*	gerechtfertigt
of course	natürlich	*powerful*	mächtig
series	Serie	*destroy*	zerstören
wave	Welle	*village*	Dorf
travel	reisen	*forest*	Wald
single	einzeln	*palm tree*	Palme
giant	riesig	*warning sign*	Warnzeichen
rush	rasen	*create*	entstehen lassen
towards	auf ... zu	*withdraw*	sich zurückziehen
coast	Küste	*unexpectedly*	unerwartet
distance	Entfernung	*surprised*	überrascht
pile up	sich auftürmen	*deadly*	tödlich
cause	hervorrufen	*hit*	treffen
earthquake	Erdbeben	*escape*	Flucht / Entrinnen

1. F (It's a series of waves or one giant wave.)
2. F (near the coast)
3. T
4. T
5. F (deep down in the ocean)
6. T
7. F (Sometimes they arrive unexpectedly.)
8. F (Not all earthquakes create a tsunami.)
9. T
10. T
11. F (Escape is nearly impossible.)

70 Listen to the interview with Mr Liam Mills, a mountain climber and mountain guide, and **circle** (kreise ein) **T** (True) or **F** (False):

Moderator: In our weekly programme *Safe Leisure* I'd like to welcome the famous mountain climber and mountain guide Liam Mills. Good evening, Mr Mills.

Mr Mills: Good evening and thank you for the invitation.

Moderator: Mr Mills, there are so many accidents in the mountains. Who is to blame for that?

Mr Mills: Mostly the hikers and tourists themselves.

Moderator: What are their biggest mistakes?

Mr Mills: Well, one big mistake is to go into the mountains without good equipment.

Moderator: What do you need for a tour in the mountains?

Mr Mills: First of all, never start a tour without your mobile phone.

Moderator: But if there is no signal in the mountains?

Mr Mills: You can always make an emergency call. Then, you need warm clothes, a rain jacket and a cap or a wooly hat even if you start your tour in fine and warm weather. You know, the weather can change very quickly in the mountains. Then, don't forget your sunglasses. And of course you must wear good shoes. Alpine boots are better than trainers and sandals are absolutely forbidden in the mountains. You also need water, food and a good sun cream with a high sun protection factor.

Moderator: Do you also wear a helmet?

Mr Mills: Yes, I do, but only if I go rock climbing. For climbing you need some special equipment like, for example, ropes, pitons and some chalk.

Moderator: Some hikers think they are fit enough for a tour and then they get into trouble.

Mr Mills: Yes, that happens again and again. Most accidents occur because people overestimate their abilities. So, before you start a tour you should get some information about the mountain. For example, how much altitude difference you will have to manage or if the tour will be easy or difficult or if there will be passages where you will have to climb. If you suffer from a fear of heights you should choose an easier route. Look out for alpine huts where you can get food or shelter. And tell somebody where you are going so that you might be found in case of an accident. But the best plan is to go with a friend or a guide.

Moderator: I'd like to thank you very much for all your helpful information. Let's hope that there won't be as many accidents as this year in the future.

Mr Mills: Yes, let's hope so.

safe	sicher	*protection factor*	Schutzfaktor
leisure	Freizeit	*helmet*	Helm
famous	berühmt	*rope*	Seil
mountain guide	Bergführer	*piton*	Kletterhaken
invitation	Einladung	*chalk*	Kreide
accident	Unfall	*trouble*	Schwierigkeit
blame for	Schuld geben	*happen*	passieren
mostly	hauptsächlich	*occur*	geschehen
hiker	Wanderer	*overestimate*	überschätzen
mistake	Fehler	*ability*	Fähigkeit
equipment	Ausrüstung	*altitude difference*	Höhenunterschied
emergency call	Notruf	*suffer from*	leiden an
wool(l)y hat	Haube	*fear of heights*	Höhenangst
even if	sogar wenn	*choose*	wählen
of course	natürlich	*alpine hut*	Berghütte
alpine boot	Wanderschuh	*shelter*	Schutz
forbidden	verboten	*in case of*	im Falle von

1. F (the hikers)
2. T
3. F (An emergency call is always possible.)
4. F (You have to take warm clothes with you because the weather can change quickly.)
5. T
6. T
7. F (A helmet is only for rock climbing.)
8. T
9. T
10. T

Listen to Mason talking about survival stories and **circle** (kreise ein) **T** (True) or **F** (False):

Hi, I'm Mason Locklear and I'm into survival stories. So, I really adore the story of Robinson Crusoe. I read the book several times. It's the story of a castaway. He spends nearly 30 years on a desert island after his shipwreck in a heavy storm. He, two cats and a dog are the only survivors. Before the ship sinks he is able to get important things like weapons, food and other useful tools from the wreck. He makes the island his home. He finds a cave and builds a fence around it. In order to survive he hunts and grows rice and corn from the grains he found on the ship. I also like the film *Cast Away* a lot. Tom Hanks plays the part of Chuck Noland, a castaway. He, too, is stranded on an uninhabited island, but after a plane crash. I'm not so much interested in the rescue part but I really like the scenes when Chuck tries to make fire or spear fish. I saw the film three times. I also saw Treasure Island on TV and I read the book. The hero dresses in goat skin. There are so many authors who write about castaways suffering loneliness and struggling to survive. I always get such books for my birthdays or at Christmas. When I'm older, I'd like to spend my holidays in a survival camp. There you learn how to build bridges out of twigs and branches, how to build shelter, how to make water clean, how to make fire, how to feed on the things nature provides, how to make clothes and much more. Yes, that's my plan for the future.

be into	sehr gerne mögen	*grain*	Korn
survival	Überleben	*stranded*	gestrandet
adore	vergöttern	*uninhabited*	unbewohnt
several	einige	*plane crash*	Flugzeugabsturz
castaway	Schiffbrüchiger	*rescue*	Rettung
desert	einsam	*spear*	aufspießen
shipwreck	Schiffbruch	*Treasure Island*	Schatzinsel
survivor	Überlebender	*goat skin*	Ziegenhaut
weapon	Waffe	*suffer*	leiden
useful	nützlich	*loneliness*	Einsamkeit
tool	Werkzeug	*struggle*	kämpfen
wreck	Wrack	*twig*	Zweig
cave	Höhle	*branch*	Ast
fence	Zaun	*shelter*	Unterschlupf
grow	anbauen	*provide*	liefern / bieten

1. T
2. T
3. F (Two cats and a dog are alive, too.)
4. T

5. T
6. T
7. F (He isn't interested in the rescue part.)
8. T

72 Listen to the phone-in programme *Speak Out* and **circle** (kreise ein) **T** (True) or **F** (False):

Moderator: Good evening to all our listeners. This is our weekly phone-in programme *Speak Out*. Our first caller is Matilda. Matilda, tell us your problem.

Matilda: Well, my problem is very difficult. It's our family holiday. My parents' ideal holiday is doing absolutely nothing. They like staying at home, sitting in the garden, listening to birds and bees. They like to read in the shade under a tree. They are into crime stories, so they always buy lots of books. But I am bored at home. I want to do something exciting. I'd like to spend my holidays at the beach swimming and surfing or in the mountains hiking and climbing. I'd prefer a holiday with activities. My dilemma is that I can't talk to them about it. They might be sad if I told them. What can I do?

Moderator: If you have got an answer to Matilda's problem, please phone now.

Toby: My name is Toby and I'd like to come up with a solution. Mathilda, you could go to a youth camp together with a friend. Your parents won't be offended if you tell them about your idea. At a youth camp there's a lot of activities for you. And it's never boring there. I was at one myself three times. You can join in sports activities like canoeing, mountain biking or rafting. You can participate in a rope climbing course or do rock climbing. You can choose whatever you like.

Moderator: Thank you, Toby, for calling. I think that's a brilliant idea.

listener	Zuhörer	*sad*	traurig
caller	Anrufer	*come up with*	sich einfallen lassen
difficult	schwierig	*solution*	Lösung
shade	Schatten	*offended*	beleidigt
be into	gerne mögen	*join in*	teilnehmen an
crime story	Krimi	*canoeing*	Kanu fahren
bored	gelangweilt	*rafting*	Wildwasser fahren
exciting	aufregend	*participate*	teilnehmen
hiking	wandern	*rope*	Seil
holiday with activities	Aktivurlaub	*choose*	auswählen
dilemma	Zwangslage	*brilliant*	großartig
might	könnte vielleicht		

1. F (They don't go on holiday, they stay at home.)
2. T
3. T
4. F (They like crime stories.)
5. T
6. T
7. T
8. T
9. F (He was there three times.)
10. T

73 Listen to the phone-in programme *Speak Out* and **circle** (kreise ein) **T** (True) or **F** (False):

Moderator: Good evening to all our <u>listeners</u>. Thank you for <u>joining</u> me on our weekly phone-in programme *Speak Out*. Our first <u>caller</u> is Amanda. Amanda, what's your problem?

Amanda: My problem is my brother. I'm really <u>worried</u> about him. <u>He used to be</u> a nice brother and a good pupil but since he made these two new friends, school is not important for him anymore and pupils who like to study are <u>nerds</u>. I'm a nerd, too because I want to have good marks. He's so <u>mean</u> to me and he's always <u>picking on me</u>. And we don't play with each other any more. His new friends <u>dropped out</u> of school but in his eyes they're cool. It's always "Harvey and Taylor do this, Harvey and Taylor do that." I can't hear that any longer. My parents have talked to my brother again and again. He has <u>promised</u> to do better but nothing has changed. When he comes home he <u>smells</u> of cigarettes and alcohol. He's so <u>disgusting</u>. Last week I went into his room because I wanted to borrow a <u>USB flash drive</u>. <u>Among</u> his exercise books I saw a small bag full of marihuana. I asked him about the bag but he told me I should <u>mind my own business</u> and threw me out of his room. I'm so worried and I don't know what to do. Should I tell my parents about it?

Moderator: This is a really big <u>dilemma</u>, Amanda. But before I ask our next caller for her <u>advice</u>, let me tell you that you have to talk to your parents. This is my personal <u>opinion</u>. And <u>on the line</u> is Mrs Warner. Good evening, Mrs Warner.

Mrs Warner: Good evening. Amanda, you'll have to inform your parents <u>immediately</u>. If you don't, it might be too late for your brother. And I think your parents will need help, too.

Moderator: I'd like to thank all our callers and goodbye until next Friday.

listener	Zuhörer	*disgusting*	widerlich
join	dabeisein	*USB flash drive*	USB-Stick
caller	Anrufer	*among*	unter
worried	besorgt	*mind my own business*	mich um meine eigenen
he used to be	er war früher		Angelegenheiten kümmern
nerd	Sonderling / Streber	*dilemma*	Zwangslage
mean	gemein	*advice*	Rat
pick on somebody	auf jem. herumhacken	*opinion*	Meinung
drop out	aufhören mit	*on the line*	in der Leitung
promise	versprechen	*immediately*	sofort / auf der Stelle
smell	riechen		

1.	T	6.	T
2.	T	7.	T
3.	T	8.	T
4.	F (He is mean to her.)	9.	F (They tell her she should inform her parents.)
5.	F (They have talked with him again and again.)		

74 Listen to the teenagers' holiday plans and **fill in the missing words:**

Sue: What are you going to do during your holidays, Raymond?
Raymond: I'm going to work at an <u>ice cream parlour</u>.
Sue: Why is that?
Raymond: Because I need to <u>earn</u> some extra money. I'm <u>saving</u> up for a new mountain bike, you know.
Sue: Great! And how long will you be working?
Raymond: For three weeks.
Sue: Then I'm going to come round and buy an ice cream there.
Raymond: Fine. What are you going to do during the summer?
Sue: The first two weeks I'm going to spend in Italy with my family. We're going to stay at a <u>campsite</u>.
Raymond: <u>Sounds</u> good!
Sue: And then I'm going to stay at home for four weeks. We could do something together if you want to.
Raymond: Perfect!
Sue: We could go and try the new <u>climbing wall</u> at the sports centre.
Raymond: Yes, I'd love to! Then we could build a tree house in our garden. My dad has already bought wood and <u>nails</u>. He's going to help us. And at the end of August I'm going to have a garden party for my birthday. Of course, you and some friends will be <u>invited</u>. And there will be a special <u>guest</u>: Liam! Hey, <u>what's the matter</u> with you? You've <u>turned all red</u> in the face! Is there a little <u>secret</u> I should know?
Sue: Ah. I must <u>confess</u>, I like Liam a lot!
Raymond: I know. That's why I'm going to invite him.
Sue: You are a really good friend, Raymond. <u>Big hug</u>!

ice cream parlour	Eissalon	*invited*	eingeladen
earn	verdienen	*guest*	Gast
save	sparen	*What's the matter?*	Was ist los?
campsite	Campingplatz	*turn all red*	ganz rot werden
sound	klingen	*secret*	Geheimnis
climbing wall	Kletterwand	*confess*	zugeben
nail	Nagel	*Big hug!*	Ich drück dich ganz fest!

1. Raymond is going to work at an **ice cream parlour**.
2. He is **saving** up for a new mountain bike.
3. Sue's going to spend two weeks at a **campsite**.
4. Then she's **going to stay** at home for four weeks.
5. They want to try the new **climbing wall** at the sports centre.
6. Then they are going to **build a tree house** in Raymond's garden.
7. His father has already bought **wood and nails** for the house.
8. At the end of August there will be a **garden / birthday party**.
9. He is going to **invite** Sue, some friends, and Liam.
10. Sue has **turned all red** in the face because she likes Liam a lot.